South Africa in Namibia: The Botha Strategy

ROBERT S. JASTER

South Africa
in Namibia:
The Botha Strategy

ROBERT S. JASTER

UNIVERSITY PRESS OF AMERICA
LANHAM • NEW YORK • LONDON

**THE CENTER FOR
INTERNATIONAL AFFAIRS
HARVARD UNIVERSITY**

University Press of America,® Inc.

4720 Boston Way
Lanham, MD 20706

3 Henrietta Street
London WC2E 8LU England

Library of Congress Cataloging in Publication Data
Jaster, Robert S.
South Africa in Namibia.

1. Namibia--Politics and government--1946-
2. National liberation movements--Namibia.
3. Self-determination, National.   4. South Africa--
Politics and government--1978-   . 5. Botha, P. W.
(Pieter Willem)   I. Title.
DT714.J37   1985   968.8'03   85-13457
ISBN 0-8191-4683-8 (alk. paper)
ISBN 0-8191-4684-6 (pbk. :   alk. paper)

Co-published by arrangement with the
Center for International Affairs, Harvard University

The Center provides a forum for the expression of responsible views.
It does not, however, necessarily agree with them.

The Center For International Affairs Executive Committee, 1984–85

Samuel P. Huntington, *Eaton Professor of the Science of Government; Director, Center for International Affairs*

Lisa Anderson, *Director of Student Programs; Assistant Professor of Government*

Leslie H. Brown, *Director of the Fellows Program*

Seyom Brown, *Acting Director, University Consortium for Research on North America*

Richard N. Cooper, *Maurits C. Boas Professor of International Economics*

Paul M. Doty, *Mallinckrodt Professor of Biochemistry; Director, Center for Science and International Affairs*

Stephan Haggard, *Acting Director of Student Programs; Assistant Professor of Government*

Chester D. Haskell, *Executive Officer*

Douglas A. Hibbs, *Professor of Government*

Stanley Hoffmann, *C. Douglas Dillon Professor of the Civilization of France; Chairman, Center for European Studies*

Herbert Kelman, *Richard Clarke Cabot Professor of Social Ethics*

Joseph S. Nye, *Clarence Dillon Professor of International Affairs*

Dwight H. Perkins, *Harold Hitchings Burbank Professor of Political Economy; Director, Harvard Institute for International Development*

Robert D. Putnam, *Chairman, Department of Government; Professor of Government*

Louise Richardson, *Ph.D. Candidate in Government*

Sidney Verba, *Director of the University Library; Carl H. Pforzheimer University Professor*

Ezra Vogel, *Director, Program on U.S. – Japan Relations; Professor of Sociology*

The Center for International Affairs is a multidisciplinary research institution within Harvard University. Founded in 1958, the Center seeks to provide a stimulating environment for a diverse group of scholars and practitioners studying various aspects of international affairs. Its purpose is the development and dissemination of knowledge concerning the basic subjects and problems of international relations. Major Center research programs include national security affairs, U.S. relations with Europe, Japan, Africa, and other areas of the world, nonviolent sanctions in conflict and defense, international economic policy, and other critical issues. At any given time, over 160 individuals are working at the Center, including faculty members from Harvard and neighboring institutions, practitioners of international affairs, visiting scholars, research associates, post-doctoral fellows, and graduate and undergraduate student associates.

TABLE OF CONTENTS

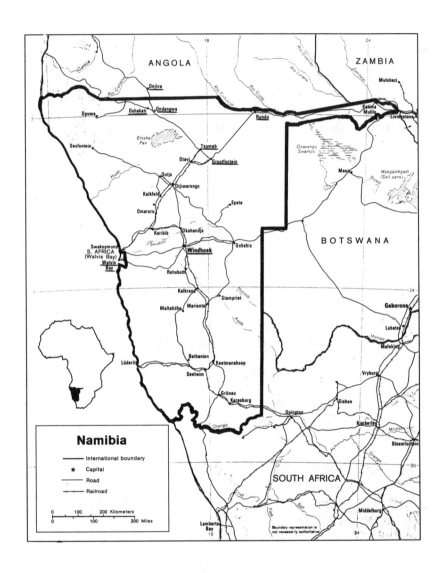

ANGOLA

ZAMBIA

Rio Cunene

Rio Cubango

Rio Cuito

Rio Cuando

Rio Linyanti

Zambezi

Mulobezi

Onjiva

Ondangwa

Rio Cunene

Katima Mulilo

Opuwa

Oshakati

Ondangwa

Rundu

Livingstone

Etosha Pan

Sesfontein

Tsumeb

Okavango Swamps

Otavi

Grootfontein

Huab

Outjo

Maun

Makgadikgadi (Salt pans)

Otjiwarongo

Kalkfeld

Epata

Omaruru

Karibib

Okahandja

Swakop

Gobabis

BOTSWANA

Swakopmund
S. AFRICA
(Walvis Bay)

Windhoek

Walvis Bay

Rehoboth

Kalkrand

Nossob

Stampriet

Maltahöhe

Marienta

Auob

Gaborone

Lobatse

Molopo

Mafeking

Bethanien

Keetmanshoop

Lüderitz

Seeheim

Vryburg

Grünau

Karasburg

Sishen

Upington

Kimberley

Modder

Oranje

Bloemfontein

30

SOUTH AFRICA

Fish

Sak

Middelburg

Lamberts Bay

Boundary representation is
not necessarily authoritative

24

18

Namibia

—— International boundary

★ Capital

— Road

—⊦— Railroad

0   100   200 Kilometers
0   100   200 Miles

* *

Chapter 1

PRELUDE TO CONFLICT: THE POLITICAL SETTING

* *

THE BROADER ISSUES

Former Vice President Mondale once remarked that, to most Americans, "Namibia" sounded like a new Baskin-Robbins ice cream flavor. As his remark suggests, that conflict is far from American consciousness. Yet it contains the seeds of a larger conflict: one that would seriously jeopardize United States interests in promoting regional security in the area.

Indeed, the Namibian conflict is the most critical of those in which southern African states recently have been engaged. No low-level bush war this, but a nasty and continuing conflict in which South Africa's preemptive war against South West Africa Peoples Organization (SWAPO)[1] guerrillas has included heavy ground and air attacks against targets deep inside SWAPO's Angolan sanctuary. Life in southern Angola has been severely disrupted by the fighting: villages abandoned or destroyed, populations uprooted, crops not grown. Casualties in this lopsided conflict have included regular Angolan troops and a few of their Soviet and Cuban advisers; probably several thousand SWAPO guerrillas and suspected SWAPO supporters, but only a small number of South Africans.

Because of the attacks on Angola, this conflict has the potential to draw outside states—particularly Cuba and the USSR—into direct armed involvement. Thus, what began as a low-key guerrilla war against South African rule in Namibia could become a messy conflict with East-West and North-South overtones. Another serious aspect,

1

particularly for the U.S., is the amount of political capital which
Washington has invested in trying to bring about an internationally
acceptable settlement. Failure to resolve the conflict will be widely
perceived, rightly or wrongly, as a failure of the Reagan
administration's policy of constructive engagement with South Africa,
and of its efforts to bend the basic peace formula (which both sides
had previously accepted in principle) in order to win a firm South
African commitment to the process.

A temporary ceasefire to which South Africa, Angola, and SWAPO
agreed early in 1984 appeared to be holding in the spring of 1985. The
ceasefire was not, however, a first stage in an agreed process for
settling the Namibia question. And while the consultative machinery
established may well facilitate moves toward permanent detente, deep
divisions remain over the two fundamental issues: the future political
configuration of Namibia and the process for arriving at a settlement.
Until these questions are resolved, the ceasefire provides only a lull in
a conflict that has been going on for eighteen years.

This study analyzes South African perceptions, goals, and strategy
in the Namibian conflict: first, because South Africa is the dominant
actor, the one with the greatest power to alter the course of the
conflict; and second, because close examination of its actions in
Namibia reveals something of the influence of ideology, party politics,
and conflicting bureaucratic interests in shaping and constraining the
policy in Namibia.

It will be argued that South African concerns over national
security, on which the military has taken a strong policy stand, have
provided only the most visible agenda for making policy decisions on
Namibia. A second major influence on South African prime minister[*]
Botha's policy has been his concern that developments in Namibia
might threaten his domestic political goals, which command a higher
priority. In particular, he has sought to avoid actions in Namibia that
might contribute to the alarming erosion of Afrikaner support for the
ruling National Party and that might threaten the chances for his
program of limited race reform at home. South African policy has

[*]Now State President

been influenced by other events as well: U.S. political developments, the Zimbabwe election results, Western pressures, and most recently, the growing costs of the insurgency, to name but a few. But domestic politics and security considerations in the broadest sense have been decisive.

Contrary to a widely held view that South Africa has pursued a strong and highly effective policy in Namibia, this study argues that, in spite of astute diplomacy and dramatic military initiatives, South African policy has been weak and irresolute. It will be shown how Botha has failed to stem the growing disarray in the Territory's internal politics, and has yet to establish an ultimate objective in Namibia or a coherent plan for a post-independence political structure.

ADMINISTRATION OF THE TERRITORY: SOUTH AFRICA VS. THE U.N.

Southwest Africa,[2] recognized as a German protectorate in 1884, fell to South African forces in 1915. When the League of Nations established a mandate system for ex-German territories following World War I, Southwest Africa was placed under the Union of South Africa as a Class "C" Mandate: i.e., to be governed as an integral part of South Africa. The United Nations Charter of 1945 provided for U.N. trusteeships to administer all the mandates, since the League was about to declare itself defunct.

South Africa, alone of the mandatory states, refused to transfer its mandate to the U.N. trusteeship system, asserting that the overwhelming majority of SWA inhabitants favored direct incorporation into South Africa. The U.N. General Assembly (UNGA) rejected Pretoria's formal request to incorporate the territory, recommending instead that South Africa agree to U.N. trusteeship. South Africa's response was to declare that it would continue to administer the Territory according to the terms of the original mandate. Thus began a political and legal battle between South Africa and the U.N. which has gone on for more than thirty years.

The General Assembly first took the issue to the International
Court of Justice (ICJ) in 1949. In its 1950 Advisory (i.e., non-binding)
Opinion the court found that: the mandate survived, and with it South
Africa's obligation; the League's supervisory functions were to be
exercised by the U.N.; South Africa was not obligated to place SWA
under the trusteeship system; South Africa could alter the Territory's
administrative status only with U.N. consent; and in any dispute over
implementing the mandate, the court's jurisdiction was binding on South
Africa.[3]

Although this opinion complicated the Territory's administrative
status, it gave both sides a legal basis on which to pursue their
opposing claims to authority. The U.N. General Assembly's increasing
concern with the SWA issue paralleled the growing criticism of
apartheid race legislation, which South Africa's newly installed (1948)
National Party government began to carry out systematically at home
and in Southwest Africa. From 1950 on, a succession of UNGA
committees was established to arrange with South Africa for U.N.
supervision of SWA. Since Pretoria's leadership from the start rejected
the notion of U.N. supervision, these committees made no headway at
all. In 1966, the General Assembly declared that South Africa had
violated the terms of its mandate by "failing to insure the material
and moral well-being . . . of the indigenous inhabitants," and that the
Mandate was therefore terminated. At the same time, it set up the
U.N. Council for Namibia to take over supervision of Southwest
Africa. The South Africans have of course refused to recognize the
Council's authority, or to allow it to enter the Territory. The Council
nonetheless has an administrative apparatus, issues visas for Namibia,
and attends international conferences in the name of Namibia.

Meanwhile, South Africa continued to carry out its own policy in
the Territory. Until the late 1960s, the thrust of that policy was in
one direction: to make Southwest Africa a de facto, and ultimately a
de jure, fifth province of South Africa. In 1949, South Africa, which
at that time was a member of the British Commonwealth, had removed
the major legislative powers over the Territory from the

British-appointed governor-general and transferred them to the South African Parliament. At the same time, Southwest Africa's whites, comprising roughly ten percent of the population at that time, were given the right to elect six representatives to the Parliament in Pretoria. In 1954, responsibility for "native" affairs. was taken from local white administration and turned over to South Africa's Minister of Bantu Administration and Development.

The first important response to external pressure came in 1962. Stung by public testimony given to the U.N. on social and economic conditions in Namibia, the government appointed the Odendaal Commission "to inquire thoroughly into further promoting the material and moral welfare and the social progress of the inhabitants of Southwest Africa, and more particularly its non-white inhabitants."[4] The Commission's recommendations centered on a five-year plan for social and economic development, and sweeping changes in the Territory's underlying political and administrative framework. First, since the continued administration of SWA as an integral part of South Africa was seen as decisive to the Territory's future development, the Commission recommended that virtually all those administrative functions still under local control (e.g., education) be removed from SWA's white-elected Legislative Assembly and taken over by the South African government. Second, regarding the Territory's future constitutional development, the Commission came out firmly against establishing a single multi-racial authority. Arguing that the most feasible and conflict-free course of political development lay in the separate development of SWA's dozen ethnic groups, the Commission laid the basis for the formal extension of South Africa's black homelands policy, or "grand apartheid," to Southwest Africa. The question of independence was not at issue.

Originally, South Africa's leaders had viewed the process of black political advancement as a long period of white guardianship and tutelage. But in 1966, encouraged by a second World Court advisory ruling which went against the U.N.[5] and spurred by growing pressures from the U.N. General Assembly, South Africa accelerated plans to

tighten control over Territorial affairs and to establish the
administrative and political division of SWA's blacks in ten separate
ethnic units. In October 1966, a couple of months after the ICJ
ruling, the General Assembly created an ad hoc Committee for
Southwest Africa specifically charged with recommending practical
steps for achieving SWA self-determination and independence.[6] In a
clear bid to undermine the UNGA initiative, the South African
government a few months later announced that it had accepted a
petition submitted three years earlier by the traditional chiefs of the
Ovambo people asking the government to move them toward
self-government. Thus, Ovamboland, a vast area stretching to the
Angolan border and incorporating the forty-five percent of SWA's
population who are Ovambo-speakers, was marked as the first of the
planned self-governing ethnic areas.[7]

In 1971, however, the International Court handed down a third and
stunning advisory opinion on Namibia. It declared that South Africa's
application of apartheid to Namibia violated its Mandate over the
Territory, thereby making its continued presence there illegal. Further,
South Africa must immediately withdraw its administration from
Namibia and U.N. member states must avoid any acts which would
have the effect of recognizing or supporting South Africa's presence.[8]

South Africa totally rejected the court's findings. Its actions
continued to be directed not at trying to accommodate the U.N.
General Assembly, but at preempting it. As Prime Minister Vorster
had told Parliament in 1968, "We shall adopt a strong attitude
[vis-a-vis the General Assembly] . . . if we show the slightest sign of
weakness, they will chase us till we can run no more. . . ."[9]

Thus, Pretoria's strategy in Namibia until 1975 was, first, to direct
the growing political aspirations of SWA blacks into local ethnic affairs
through the creation of local legislative bodies; and second, to weaken
the nascent territorial administrative and political structure of SWA as
a single entity, thereby making its inhabitants less receptive to
nationalist appeals and its local administrators less concerned with
Territory-wide issues. Meanwhile, increasingly strident UNGA demands

that Namibia be moved toward independence as an integrated whole were met with South African assurances that the two approaches were not in conflict. In May 1973, following the adoption of new legislation establishing the machinery for self-governing ethnic authorities in the Territory, Vorster assured the U.N. Secretary-General that South Africa did not intend to push individual ethnic groups toward separate independence, and that it would cooperate with the Secretary-General in assisting the SWA people to attain self-determination and eventual independence, which Vorster believed could occur within ten years.[10] His lack of commitment to a unitary state was evident in his simultaneous assurances to Parliament that ultimately the Territory's people would have "to decide if they want confederation or a unitary state and those who want to opt out can opt out."[11] (Emphasis added.)

In 1972, however, two significant South African concessions went almost unnoticed. In September, Vorster received a special representative of the U.N. Secretary-General, thus marking the start of direct negotiations between South Africa and the U.N. over the Territory. And on 20 November, a speech by Vorster made it clear that the government had formally abandoned the notion of annexation.[12] But on the key issue of taking steps to move the Territory toward independence, South Africa continued to stall. This led the Security Council to break off the Secretary-General's talks with Vorster and to threaten South Africa with sanctions if it failed by 30 March 1975 to comply with the council's demands that South Africa withdraw and turn over political power to the Namibian people.[13]

THE TURNHALLE INITIATIVE

By the spring of 1975, the U.N. was not the only source of mounting pressure on the Vorster policy in Namibia, however. The Territory's 72,000 whites—for the most part Afrikaners with ultra-conservative views on racial matters and with strong political connections to South Africa's ruling National Party—were concerned that the government might be preparing to cave in to U.N. demands. To allay their anxiety, Vorster declared in Parliament[14] that he had "every confidence in the future of Southwest Africa." Anyone "who disposes of his property there because he is afraid of the future of Southwest Africa is harming . . . himself [and] the Territory as well." He hoped that people would not take fright, but would do everything to develop the territory, and would "in fact entrench themselves more firmly there." Then he addressed their fears directly:

> What is making people afraid is the story that Southwest Africa will be handed over to Sam Nujoma and his [SWAPO] people . . . But in view of the clear standpoint of South Africa in respect of SWAPO and Sam Nujoma, there is not need at all for people to be panic-stricken over that aspect of the matter, particularly [because] Southwest Africa can never mean anything in the world without the cooperation of South Africa.

The accession to power of a self-declared Marxist national movement in Mozambique and the growing civil war in Angola, in which South Africa was soon to play a fateful role, were additional sources of South African concern over Southwest Africa in 1975. In June, only a Western veto prevented the U.N. Security Council from formally calling for punitive measures against South Africa to force its withdrawal from the Territory. Added to this was a growing number of political assassinations and other violent actions by SWAPO.

Faced with these pressures, Vorster decided on a bold new course. In September 1975, a Constitutional Conference was convened at the Turnhalle building in Windhoek, SWA's capital. Its mandate was to draw up a constitution, following which an interim government would be established to lead Namibia to independence. The invited delegates were the moderate leaders of Southwest Africa's eleven official ethnic groups, including whites. Political parties were not represented, nor was SWAPO invited to take part.

Vorster's objectives with the Turnhalle initiative appear to have been to head off U.N. sanctions by agreeing to Namibia's independence, while making sure that Pretoria, not the U.N., controlled the process; further, to preempt growing demands by Namibian blacks for a voice in Territorial affairs, while assuring that black political activity would take place largely within the confines of each of the official ethnic communities.

For the next eighteen months, the Turnhalle delegates worked on constitutional and other issues. During this same period, the South African government conferred various degrees of self-government on six ethnic communities.[15] By March 1977, the Turnhalle group had completed a draft constitution providing for a multi-ethnic, three-tier legislature. The first tier, a sixty-member national assembly, would handle such national matters as defense and foreign affairs. Its members were to be appointed by the second tier: the representative bodies (legislative assemblies, tribal councils, etc.) of the eleven recognized population groups. The third tier would be made up of local (municipal) councils. The second and third tiers would have authority over such important local matters as housing, education, health, etc. This arrangement would guarantee the whites control over their own communities, and would assure the various ethnic groups that the future government would not be dominated by the Ovambo people, who account for almost half of the population. The Turnhalle constitutional committee further recommended that an interim government be established and that independence be set for the end of 1978.

The main points to note about the Turnhalle initiative are that it was a process which the Vorster government set in motion and to which it was committed; and it held promise of imminent (if not complete) independence for the Territory as well as substantial political power for the ethnic leaders who were engaged in the Turnhalle process. Thus, local political hopes and ambitions were aroused which were to be dashed two years later at some cost.

THE CONTACT GROUP'S DEMARCHE

Pressure on South Africa continued to build during 1976. The African states enlarged their constituency calling for economic sanctions. The Security Council unanimously adopted Resolution 385, which set out the conditions for U.N.-managed elections. On 7 April 1977, only three weeks after the Turnhalle Constitutional Conference had approved the draft constitution, the Security Council's five Western members (the U.S., Canada, Britain, France, and West Germany) delivered a strong note to Prime Minister Vorster, once again condemning South African activities in Namibia and demanding free elections, withdrawal of South African forces, and release of political detainees. The note also demanded that the Turnhalle plans for an interim government be dropped.

Two months of intensive private talks between this unofficial Western "Contact Group," led by the U.S. ambassador to the U.N., Donald McHenry, and South African leaders brought dramatic results. By late April, Vorster had agreed to end apartheid in the territory and to support free elections in which SWAPO would take part, provided the West did not press for an early South African withdrawal. Further discussions of the Contact Group with the internal Namibian parties and Vorster during May brought agreement to cancel plans to establish an interim Turnhalle government. On 10 June the Turnhalle delegation, following discussions with Vorster, formally requested him to cancel its request for an interim government, and agreed instead to his appointment of a South African administrator-general who would prepare the territory for elections to a constituent assembly and govern the territory in the interim. Parliament immediately passed a bill permitting the enactment, repeal, and amendment of SWA regulations and the appointment of an administrator-general.

Vorster told Parliament that this would pave the way for the election of a constituent assembly and would eventually "make the territory in its entirety independent."[16] He explained the need for this abrupt reversal of policy in terms of outside pressure: Turnhalle, he said, had reached a consensus on how the territory "should become independent without one group dominating the others." This was a "remarkable achievement," but, while "one would have thought they would be applauded from all sides, especially by the Western powers . . . unfortunately they received, to put it at its highest, only lukewarm reception." Moreover, he said, the Turnhalle leaders would like to have the world recognize their independence; they were afraid that, had they gone ahead with an interim government, it would have prejudiced their international acceptance.[17] Vorster also hinted at some of the difficulties this reversal of policy entailed, noting that many existing laws would have to be repealed and new legislation introduced, particularly since parts of the territory had been "virtually self-governing." The disappointment of local politicians who, for the two years of Turnhalle, believed they were destined to dispense real political power, contributed to the dissension and bitterness that have continued to dominate internal Namibian politics.

In September, the government's commitment to an independent and unitary Namibia was reinforced with the passage of a parliamentary bill by which the enclave of Walvis Bay—Namibia's only deep-water port and the site of a major South African military training base—was formally annexed to South Africa.[18] At the same time, South Africa installed Judge Marthinus Steyn as Administrator-General of the Territory.

The next nine months were a brief and troubled honeymoon for South Africa and the Western Contact Group. Some important mutual accommodation occurred. The Administrator-General quickly repealed several major pieces of apartheid legislation in the Territory and relaxed racial restrictions on property ownership and residence rights. So-called "proximity talks," in which the Contact Group met separately with SWAPO and South African officials in New York, substantially narrowed the range of contentious issues and the differences between the two sides. They agreed in principle on the following: a special U.N. representative and a U.N. planning group to run Namibia during a transition period; a ceasefire calling for withdrawal and restriction of both armed forces to specified locations; and a U.N.-supervised election to a constituent assembly to occur by the end of 1978.

In early February 1978, however, the South Africans broke off the talks, charging that the terms being offered would result in the Territory's being "overrun and governed by Marxist terrorists."[19] The South Africans particularly objected to SWAPO's demand that Walvis Bay be designated in advance a part of Namibia—an issue the South Africans insisted should be negotiated later with an independent Namibia—and to SWAPO's refusal to permit its bases in Angola to be subject to U.N. monitoring during the ceasefire. On 14 February, Foreign Minister Roelof Botha emerged, flushed and angry, from a long and apparently acrimonious cabinet meeting, following which Vorster announced that South Africa would carry out its own plan for internal elections in Namibia and unilateral independence by year's end.[20] Hard-liners, presumably led by (then) Defence Minister P. W. Botha, had won the day.

The next couple of months saw growing violence in the Territory. SWAPO launched a campaign of kidnappings and assassinations of local political leaders, prompting South African authorities to institute sweeping powers of arrest and detention. External pressures and the threat of sanctions—pressures which had induced Vorster to make past concessions—were also growing.

These developments were probably chiefly responsible for Vorster's turnabout in April. On 25 April, South Africa announced its acceptance of "clarified" settlement terms, which the Contact Group had offered in late March. In fact, the new terms were not markedly different from the old. Walvis Bay would be excluded from the settlement, but the Western Five promised SWAPO to support its claim following independence. South Africa's acceptance was conditional, however: a reduced South African security force must be allowed to remain in Namibia following independence if invited to do so by the constituent assembly; all hostilities must end prior to a South African troop withdrawal; and South Africa must be responsible for maintaining law and order during the transition.

In addition, South Africa insisted that the latest proposals, together with its new demands, be agreed on as final and not subject to further negotiation or change. This last stipulation suggests that the decision to accept the Western proposals was hard-fought within the top leadership, and that the "soft-liners" prevailed only by accepting strict limitations on the government's freedom of maneuver in future negotiations. Further sops to the hard-liners were the government's arrest of nine members of SWAPO's legal internal wing, and the launching of South Africa's first deep penetration raid into Angola. The arrests took place on 25 April, the same day South Africa announced its acceptance of the Western peace formula. Nine days later South Africa launched an airborne attack on a SWAPO base camp at Cassinga (250 kilometers inside Angola) which resulted in several hundred suspected SWAPO casualties. The raid led SWAPO to suspend the talks for more than a month. In mid-June, as the talks resumed, settlement prospects were given a further setback by Pretoria's announcement of plans to register Namibians for an internal election to be supervised by South Africa.

Talks languished until late summer, when U.N. Secretary-General Waldheim officially presented the U.N.'s new plan for a ceasefire, elections to a constituent assembly, adoption of a constitution, and independence. On 6 September, the South African cabinet, chaired by Defence Minister Botha in place of the ailing Vorster, formally rejected key elements of the Waldheim plan: the size of the proposed U.N. force (7,500), the postponement of elections beyond 31 December, and the replacement of local police by U.N. authorities during the transition. Two weeks later, South Africa announced that it would proceed to hold internal Namibian elections before the year's end.

Although South African officials have since said in private conversations that the spring of 1978 had been the most opportune moment for a settlement, this seems to be a case of 20-20 hindsight. They expressed the belief that an immediate election might have caught SWAPO unprepared and less able to intimidate voters than one held after an extended pre-election campaign. It is probably true that this was as close as South Africa would come to accepting the terms of an internationally acceptable settlement during seven years of talks. But South Africa's aggressive military stance at the time, together with its hasty moves to put an internal settlement in train in the latter half of 1978, showed that its leaders were not agreed on the necessity of seeking a settlement that the world would recognize.

By October of that year, when the Western Five Contact Group made its next demarche to Pretoria, they were dealing with a new administration there. Vorster, who had earlier made a number of concessions in response to Western pressure, had stepped down as Prime Minister in favor of P. W. Botha, his hard-line Minister of Defence.

NOTES

1. The South West Africa Peoples Organization is an Ovambo-dominated national movement, Christian in background and generally Marxist in political orientation.

2. The name "Namibia" is apparently preferred by the territory's blacks and is derived from the great Namib coastal desert. South African authorities retain the old German protectorate name, Southwest Africa (SWA).

3. For a more detailed discussion of these issues, see John Wellington, South West Africa and Its Human Issues (Oxford: Clarendon Press, 1967), pp. 329ff; and A Trust Betrayed: Namibia (New York: U.N. Office of Public Information, 1974).

4. Wellington, South West Africa, p. 376.

5. Formally, the Court held that the two applicants, Ethiopia and Liberia, had no legal status or right to question South African performance in SWA. By implication, the decision appeared to weaken the U.N.'s claim to supervisory powers over the Territory and its arguments against the application of apartheid there. See "The South Africa Case: What Happened?" by Ernest Gross in Foreign Affairs, October 1966; and Southwest Africa Survey 1967, RSA Department of Foreign Affairs, March 1967, pp. 36-37.

6. UNGA, 21st Session, Res. No. 2145 (XXI), 27 October 1966.

7. Southwest Africa Survey 1967, RSA Department of Foreign Affairs, March 1967; New York Times, 2 March 1967.

8. See U.N. Office of Public Information, A Trust Betrayed: Namibia.

9. Cited in Amry Vandenbosch, South Africa and the World (Lexington, Kentucky: University of Kentucky Press, 1970), p. 224.

10. D. S. Prinsloo, Southwest Africa/Namibia: Toward a Negotiated Settlement (Pretoria: Foreign Affairs Association, 1977).

11. South Africa, House of Assembly Debates, 28 February 1973, col. 1697.

12. See G. Totemeyer, South West Africa/Namibia: Facts, Attitudes, Assessments, and Prospects (Randburg: Folks Suid Publishers, 1977).

13. UNSC Resolution 366, 17 December 1974.

14. South Africa, House of Assembly Debates 1975, vol. 56, cols. 4512-3.

15. Three—the Ovambo, Kavango, and Caprivi—had legislative councils, while the Bushmen, Namas, and Damaras each had an intermediate degree of self-government. See Namibia: The Constitutional Fraud, International Defence and Aid Fund Briefing Paper No. 2, July 1981.

16. South Africa, House of Assembly Debates 1977, 14 June 1977, col. 10122.

17. Ibid., cols. 10127, 10172.

18. South Africa justified this move on the basis of earlier Anglo-German treaties which had recognized Walvis Bay as a British enclave separate from Germany's SWA Protectorate. By an act of 1922, however, South Africa had established it as part of the Territory "for judicial purposes." See D. S. Prinsloo, Walvis Bay and the Penguin Islands: Background and Status, Foreign Affairs Association (SA) Study Report No. 8, November 1977; and Strategic Survey 1977 (London: International Institute for Strategic Studies, 1978), p. 38.

19. For a detailed analysis of these negotiations, see Strategic Survey 1978 (London: International Institute for Strategic Studies, 1979), pp. 85-89.

20. Private source.

* * * * * * * * * * * * * * * * * * * *

Chapter 2

THE SWAPO INSURGENCY

* * * * * * * * * * * * * * * * * * * *

The South West Africa Peoples Organization had its roots in the Ovambo labor movement of the late 1950s.[1] Founded in Capetown as the Ovambo Peoples Organization (OPO), its initial objective was to bring an end to the contract labor system in SWA. Hence, its support came largely from the Ovambo contract laborers who make up a large majority of the work force in Windhoek and Walvis Bay, the territory's two major employment centers. Its founder, Herman Toivo ja Toivo, had close working ties with South Africa's Liberal Party and with SWANU, a moderate political organization of the Herero people, and is alleged to have been in contact with the South African Communist Party as well.[2]

After repeated arrests of OPO leaders for their part in SWA labor disturbances, a number of them fled the territory. Sam Nujoma and several others went to New York, where they began to seek support for the OPO among U.N. delegates. Early on, however, OPO's leaders recognized the need to broaden their support base beyond the Ovambo people. With the added incentive of trying to win U.N. recognition, it was essential to campaign as a national organization. Thus, in 1960, SWAPO came into being in New York. The genesis of SWAPO is significant in light of the official South African view of its origins, which is discussed at greater length below.

Almost since its inception, SWAPO has been active diplomatically. Through effective lobbying at the U.N., SWAPO won official recognition by the General Assembly in 1973 as the "sole authentic

17

representative" of the Namibian people, even though a number of other political organizations were active in Namibia at that time. SWAPO representatives have also succeeded in obtaining substantial financial and other non-military assistance from a variety of Western (particularly Scandinavian) governments, as well as from private religious and other groups. The USSR has supplied weapons, while Cuba, East Germany, and several other Communist states have provided military instructors and training. Africa's Frontline states[3] became seriously seized of the Namibian problem in 1979-80, when the Western-led peace initiative entered full stride. SWAPO has sometimes chosen to bypass its Frontline supporters to make a direct appeal for global support of its position. In September 1980, some West European Communist parties allegedly helped SWAPO organize in Paris a 700-member Conference on Solidarity with the Namibian People, which "demanded" an end to the Western peace plan and a U.N. Security Council meeting to approve mandatory economic sanctions against South Africa.[4]

SWAPO's political program for Namibia has not been set down with consistency or in detail. Indeed, SWAPO spokesmen have offered substantially different versions, depending on the time and the particular audience. Constitutional proposals issued by SWAPO's internal wing in 1975 called for an executive president, a single-chamber legislature, an independent judiciary and a supreme court, a bill of rights, and association with the British Commonwealth. The form of economic organization would be left up to the future Namibian government.[5] But a Communist publication[6] in 1977 claimed the SWAPO program was to create a "vanguard party" and to build "a classless, non-exploitative society based on scientific socialist ideals and principles." A still more recent statement, and probably the most authoritative since the speaker was Moses Garoeb, SWAPO's Secretary-General, stressed SWAPO's pragmatism.[7] SWAPO would be committed to the rule of law, political stability, and a pragmatic economic policy. Though committed to socialism, this would not come overnight. Contracts between Pretoria and the big multinationals would be renegotiated. The ANC would not be allowed military bases in Namibia, which would seek "correct and cordial relations" with South Africa. Nor would SWAPO impose a one-party state.

These variations reflect SWAPO's major weaknesses as a national liberation movement. Because of SWAPO's dependence on outside support for its very survival, its spokesmen are inclined to express a belligerent, Marxist line when they are in Moscow seeking arms, and to take a pragmatic, nonaligned, less doctrinaire stance when they are looking for diplomatic and financial support from the Frontline states or the U.N. Beyond that, there are believed to be serious factional differences among the SWAPO leadership hierarchy. South African foreign office officials[8] identify a militant, pro-Soviet faction led by a USSR-trained guerrilla chief, and a political wing which is thought to be moderate, Christian, and non-Marxist. SWAPO president Sam Nujoma is believed to be somewhere in the middle. This view was at least partially confirmed by a SWAPO official,[9] who said that Nujoma is "a good team-worker" who helps to maintain SWAPO unity. A further and probably most compelling reason for conflicting expressions of SWAPO's plans for an independent Namibia is simply this: an insurgency which has suffered severe military setbacks, and a continuing Western-led peace initiative in which vital SWAPO interests are at risk—these issues have taken precedence among SWAPO's thin and widely scattered leadership. The definitive blueprint for Namibia's future will have to wait.

Meanwhile, SWAPO has been markedly successful in winning growing political support within Namibia and in enhancing its claim to being the leading Namibian national movement. During 1984, one important political party and leading members of at least two others deserted the major coalition opposing SWAPO and formed an alliance with SWAPO. Even the Botha government now tacitly recognizes that SWAPO cannot be denied some role in the eventual settlement and in the politics of an independent Namibia.

The insurgency itself got off to a slow and unpromising start in 1966—four years after SWAPO's leadership, seeking to gain credibility

with the U.N. as an active national-liberation movement, declared an
end to nonviolence in favor of armed revolution. A few isolated
hit-and-run attacks in northern Ovamboland in the autumn of 1966 led
quickly to a security sweep by South African police and to the
Terrorism Trials of 1967.   Thirty members of SWAPO, including its
founder, Herman Toivo ja Toivo, were tried in Pretoria and sentenced
(under a retroactive Terrorism Act)[10] to long prison terms. By the
early 1970s SWAPO had established several guerrilla bases along the
remote Caprivi-Zambian border, from which they penetrated Namibia
far enough to mine the roads patrolled by South African border
police.

Only in 1975, during the chaos in Angola following the collapse of
Portugese rule, was SWAPO able to move armed men from Tanzania
through Zambia into the southern part of Angola, where they mixed
more easily with fellow Ovambo people who spilled over both sides of
the border. They soon were infiltrating northern Namibia in larger
numbers: a skirmish in late 1975 resulted in the deaths of sixty-one
SWAPO guerrillas and three South Africans. With growing support
from Angola's MPLA government, SWAPO was causing sufficient
trouble in the spring of 1976 for the authorities to declare
quasi-emergency rule over the Ovambo, Kavango, and Caprivi areas in
which more than half of Namibia's population is located.

By late 1977, groups of SWAPO guerrillas were raiding
Ovamboland, where South African forces claimed to be intercepting
them in roughly 100 clashes a month.[11] At that time, South Africa
officially estimated SWAPO's guerrilla strength to be more than 3,500,
of whom some 300 were believed to be operating inside Namibia.[12]
South Africa took these mostly small-scale raids seriously: the clearing
of a kilometer-wide strip along the Angolan border in 1977 required
the resettlement of 3,000 Ovambos displaced from the cleared zone
and the erection of a border security fence 450 kilometers long.[13]
SWAPO hit-and-run tactics, mainly directed at assassinating moderate
black leaders in Namibia, nevertheless continued in the early part of
1978.

Indeed, neither the rapid buildup of South Africa's forces in
Namibia nor its highly aggressive counter-insurgency after 1978
prevented the growth of SWAPO's numbers and capabilities in the years
1978-82. The increasing flow of Soviet weapons and Cuban and East
German military instructors enabled SWAPO to infiltrate more
effectively and to do greater damage. In 1979, the South Africans
noted SWAPO's improved anti-tracking techniques, for example.[14]
Sabotage of power lines blacked out major Namibian towns a number
of times in 1980, while SWAPO's growing attacks on roads forced oil
tank trucks and other traffic to move across the territory in armed
convoys. Nor were military targets immune: in 1980, a SWAPO mortar
attack destroyed a number of military aircraft at South Africa's
Ondangwa base, some forty kilometers below the Angolan border. The
scale of infiltration also increased.

In the summer of 1980, South African forces began launching
frequent ground and air attacks, some of them heavy, against SWAPO
targets deep inside Angola. These preemptive attacks dealt a setback
to SWAPO, which suffered heavy casualties and substantial defections
and was forced to initiate guerrilla raids from bases as far as 200
miles above the Namibian border.[15] In early 1982, SWAPO seemed to
be reverting to its earlier tactics: assassinating tribal chiefs and other
local officials of the SWA administration while seeking to avoid
contact with South African troops. As late as March 1982, South
African intelligence officials were expressing confidence that SWAPO
would be "wiped out as a terrorist force."[16]

Yet SWAPO was far from finished. The South Africans themselves
estimated its trained guerrilla strength in 1982 as 6,000: almost double
their estimate of 1977.[17] In April 1982, a group of 100 SWAPO
guerrillas penetrated 130 miles into Namibia near the mining town of
Tsumeb. They were reported to have killed nine South African soldiers
and four civilians in a series of running actions.[18] The April
penetration also demonstrated a growing SWAPO sophistication in
combat capabilities: RPG7 rockets fired into an armored troop carrier
killed seven South African soldiers; and road mines laid in white

farming areas were, for the first time, linked together to create multiple explosions with the detonation of a single mine.[19]

These attacks did not herald the start of a new, more aggressive stage in the insurgency. South Africa's counterinsurgency and intelligence capabilities are simply too great to permit SWAPO to prepare and carry out the sort of guerrilla war that occurred in Rhodesia, where vast parts of the country came under attack and eventually passed out of the government's military and administrative control.

The April attack probably was of greater political than military importance for SWAPO. Leaders of the Frontline states, which have been an indispensable source of logistical and diplomatic support to SWAPO, had been critical of SWAPO's war efforts. They found it difficult to press with conviction SWAPO's claims as a guerrilla movement with pretensions to power while its military exploits had been limited to sporadic raids and isolated killings. Frontline engagement in SWAPO's cause has often been only lukewarm.[20]

Despite the 1,268 SWAPO deaths claimed by the South African Defence Forces (SADF) in 1982, the guerrillas launched their annual rainy-season offensive in early 1983, infiltrating 1,600 men across "a wide area," according to South African officials. An undisclosed number were still in the territory three months later.

In February 1984, South Africa, Angola, and SWAPO agreed to a ceasefire in Angola to be jointly monitored by SADF and Angolan troops. This accord, which SWAPO undoubtedly agreed to only under Angolan pressure, has already slowed its infiltration into Namibia: during the first four months of the ceasefire, South Africa reported that joint SADF-Angolan patrols had intercepted SWAPO forces thirty-three times.[21] Yet, at least in the early weeks of the accord, SWAPO was reported to have infiltrated 800 guerrillas into Namibia and to have carried out mortar attacks on a northern town and on the main SAAF base at Ondangwa.[22]

The SWAPO insurgency has not so far posed a real threat to South African authority in Namibia, nor has it seriously disrupted the territory's economic life. Yet the South African government views the insurgency as a serious threat and, as discussed elsewhere in this study, has met it with a costly and aggressive response. How, then, is SWAPO viewed by the South African leadership? In particular, what is the perceived threat? And what is at stake for South Africa in Namibia, and in the ultimate outcome of the conflict?

NOTES

1. For more detailed discussion, see G. Totemeyer, Namibia Old and New (New York: St. Martins Press, 1978); John Dugard, The South West Africa/Namibia Dispute (Berkeley: University of California Press, 1973).

2. Totemeyer, South West Africa/Namibia, p. 62.

3. The Frontline states, so designated by the Organization of African Unity because they have been the "front line" of black Africa's struggle against white minority rule, include Angola, Botswana, Mozambique, Tanzania, Zambia, and Zimbabwe.

4. From a private European source.

5. Totemeyer, South West Africa/Namibia, pp. 72-73.

6. The African Communist, No. 68, 1977, p. 12.

7. Interview in a Salisbury newspaper, quoted in the South Africa Foundation News, December 1981.

8. Private conversation in May 1981.

9. Private conversation in March 1981.

10. Dugard, South West Africa/Namibia Dispute, pp. 414ff.

11. IISS, Strategic Survey 1977, p. 39.

12. Ibid.

13. Totemeyer, Namibia Old and New, p. 128.

14. South Africa, House of Assembly Debates, April 1979,
    col. 4738.

15. IISS, Strategic Survey 1980-81, p. 90.

16. The Sun, Baltimore, 22 March 1982.

17. Ibid., citing an "SADF intelligence officer."

18. Washington Post, 22 April 1982.

19. Ibid.

20. See R. Jaster, A Regional Security Role for Africa's Frontline
    States: Experience and Prospects, Adelphi Paper No. 180,
    London, IISS, Spring 1983.

21. New York Times, 10 June 1984.

22. Ibid., 7 March 1984.

* *

Chapter 3

THE STAKES FOR SOUTH AFRICA

* *

South Africa's policy on Namibia is driven by three major concerns: the security of the republic, domestic politics, and the political situation in Namibia. The first of these has always predominated. Yet all three are closely interrelated. The leaders' perception of the security threat, and their response to it, is influenced by their calculus of how Namibia is viewed as a security issue by the South African electorate and how it will affect domestic white politics. Similarly, political developments inside Namibia bear directly on the leadership's security assessment and can easily spill over into politics within the republic itself.

Pressure from the international community and, more recently, the growing economic burden of the war have also influenced South African policy. But neither has taken precedence over security or domestic political concerns. In the final months of Vorster's administration, he seemed to have concluded that all three of South Africa's major interests in Namibia would best be served by moving toward acceptance of the Western proposals. It will be argued below, however, that the Botha government has viewed the Western Five's peace initiative as inimical to South Africa's national security and domestic political imperatives. And while Botha has complained since 1981 about the growing costs of the conflict, he has shown no inclination to settle on anything other than his own terms.

But to understand South African policies regarding Namibia, it is necessary to examine what the leadership perceives to be at stake in the conflict.

THE PERCEIVED SECURITY THREAT

The leadership's perception of events in Namibia is consistent with its strategic concept of the "total onslaught" which it sees being waged against South Africa. Indeed, the Namibian conflict is an integral element in that concept. The threat perception has several aspects, both political and military.

First, the leaders share a general conviction that Namibia is the next objective on what they see as the continuing march of international Communism through Africa toward the ultimate target: South Africa. The Mugabe electoral victory in Zimbabwe is viewed not as an exception or setback to the alleged Communist "blueprint," but as a worst-case scenario: the fall of one more domino. South Africa's long-nurtured image of Mugabe as a Marxist terrorist overshadows the clear evidence of his anti-Soviet stance. Similarly, SWAPO is seen as the thin edge of the Soviet wedge. South Africa's foreign minister, in a high-level and confidential meeting at the U.S. State Department in April 1981,[1] told Assistant Secretary of State Crocker that Nujoma had "made promises to the Soviets" and that defectors from SWAPO had revealed to the South African government the Soviet plan: "first Namibia, then Botswana, Lesotho, and Swaziland, followed by the final attack on South Africa. The Government can't ignore this reality. We wouldn't [sic] justify that to our people."

Second, South African leaders classify SWAPO and its leadership in an undifferentiated way as "Communists." Prime Minister Vorster told Parliament in 1976 that SWAPO was "conceived and born in Communist sin," and that Nujoma himself was a Communist.[2] The Botha government had adopted this same official position. Ministry of Foreign Affairs regional specialists in Pretoria speak knowledgeably in private of conservative and radical wings of SWAPO, with Nujoma somewhere near the center, and acknowledge that Lutheran chaplains accompany SWAPO units in the field.[3] Yet, South Africa's foreign minister told Crocker in private that Nujoma is "a bloody thug," and that "We're convinced that SWAPO is Marxist . . . SWAPO's people are indoctrinated in Marxism every day. [Our] bottom line is, no Moscow flag in Windhoek."[4]

It is tempting to attribute this statement to the government's belief that the Reagan administration would be responsive to any charge, no matter how simplistic, of Soviet machinations in the Third World. Although this motive doubtless has been an important element in the Botha administration's approach to the U.S., the leadership's position that the SWAPO insurgency is Soviet-inspired and controlled stems from the complex of political and historical factors going back to Communist links with white labor troubles in the 1920s and with the emergence of black resistance to apartheid more than thirty years ago. Both events led to widespread white acceptance of the proposition that South Africa's race troubles and international pariah status are due to an orchestrated Communist campaign to wrest South Africa and its mineral wealth from the West.

In any event, whether or not the leaders' official assessment of SWAPO reflects political opportunism or a deeply rooted conviction is largely irrelevant; the point is, South African policy on Namibia is based on that assessment and is entirely consistent with it. Moreover, that assessment is widely shared among South African white politicians, regardless of party affiliation, and provides the underlying framework for discussing the Namibian issue within the National Party, the government, Parliament, and the press.

What specific threats to security, then, does South Africa fear from a SWAPO and a SWAPO-dominated Namibia? Political leaders fear that a SWAPO regime would, either out of ideological conviction or obligation to its Soviet supporters, "invite the Russians and Cubans in" and give support and sanctuary to African National Congress (ANC) guerrillas operating against the Republic. Although South African officials have been cautious in saying so directly, they also appear concerned that a radical black-ruled Namibia would serve as a model and stimulus for black opposition leaders within the Republic itself. Thus, Pretoria's foreign and defense ministers, in a joint interview with a leading Afrikaans newspaper,[5] warned that a South African withdrawal from Namibia would, among other damaging results, "contribute in a high degree to the intensification of the revolutionary climate and . . . fill the conservative elements among all the population groups with a spirit of defeatism."

The Foreign Minister was even more blunt in private conversation with Crocker: "Nujoma will nationalize the whole place, and cause upheaval and civil war, involving South Africa. We will have to invade Namibia and other countries as well."[6]

Military leaders have been equally explicit in defining the threat. Defense chief Malan, at the same meeting with Crocker in April 1981, is reported in the private minutes of the talks to have "flatly declared" that "the SAG can't accept prospects of a SWAPO victory which brings Soviet/Cuban forces to Walvis Bay. This would result from any election which left SWAPO in a dominant position. Therefore a SWAPO victory would be unacceptable in the context of a Westminster-type political system."[7] (Emphasis added.)

This hardline position, which represents a clear backing off from South African commitments made in 1978, has been reiterated by the military spokesmen in public. A commodore and a colonel representing the SADF told a prestigious and conservative congress on racial matters held in Pretoria in 1982 that there would be no repetition of the "Zimbabwe fiasco" in Southwest Africa, which "could never accept a Lancaster House-type of agreement, or elections under conditions laid down by the U.N."[8] This, too, represents a retreat from commitments in principle made under the Vorster administration.

South Africa's military leaders are also concerned that an independent Namibia might be used as a springboard for a conventional attack on the Republic. Namibian geography alone would seem to make this a remote contingency, even under the most extreme assumptions; yet a large-scale military exercise which the SADF conducted in 1977 tested a mechanized combat group in conventional warfare against an "enemy" armored division entering the Republic from southern Namibia at a point near the town of Upington.[9]

Concern over a future conventional attack is linked to defense officials' alarm at the presence of foreign military personnel in southern Angola. In 1979, H. M. J. Coetzee, South Africa's Deputy Defense Minister, claimed there were 4,000 to 6,000 East German troops "deployed" in Angola and Mozambique, and that units of this "Afrika Corps" were preparing to intervene directly in the SWAPO insurgency.[10] Although this did not happen and the East Germans (numbering perhaps as high as 1,500, according to Western intelligence officials) have limited their activities to weapons training, the South African fear of foreign intervention nevertheless remains strong. Following South Africa's major raid into Angola in August/September 1981, Defence Minister Malan told Parliament that "a disturbing aspect of this operation was that there were Russians everywhere, even along our borders . . . I do not know what the Russians were engaged in doing."[11] Nor is this view limited to SADF leaders. In 1979, an opposition MP urged an increase in the size of South Africa's permanent defense force because

> . . . in Africa as things stand we are not going to have to deal with a purely African situation . . . we must unfortunately expect to see more foreign troops on our borders. [We already have the Cubans; now something new has been added]: a second Africa Corps . . . composed of East Germans . . . highly trained and experienced . . . paratroopers equipped with the most modern weapons, who are poised to the north of South West Africa.[12]

At the tactical level, SADF officials have been concerned about the growing sophistication of SWAPO as a fighting force and about the dangers of its opening a second front. Evidence of improved technical and tactical capabilities has been attributed directly to the presence of Soviet and East German military specialists. Fear of a second front revived in the spring of 1982, following a suprise SWAPO raid launched from the extreme southwest corner of Angola. In April 1982, General Lloyd, chief of the Southwest Africa Territorial Forces at that time, said the attack revealed SWAPO's plan to extend the fighting to

Kaokoland, then farther south into Damaraland.[13]

Within the higher echelons of South Africa's military establishment, differences of opinion and some frictions have emerged over Namibia. In part, this appears to reflect the normal sort of bureaucratic friction found in any military hierarchy.[14]

There are also thought to be differences over specific policy issues on Namibia, generally drawn along verkrampte-verligte lines (i.e., status quo Afrikaners vs. those favoring modest race reform). One such difference is a basic question of defense strategy: whether the Cunene or the Orange is the better defensive line. Some Western analysts report that senior SADF officers have asserted in private that, from a purely military standpoint, the Orange River line, with hundreds of miles of virtually uninhabited, treeless, Namibian desert to its north, would be far easier to defend than the more distant, populous, and bush-covered Cunene River area lying along the Angola-Namibia border. Yet an SADF general officer recently told the author that he was astonished at such a proposition: "Never in my career have I heard a South African military man assert that the Orange is a better defense line than the Cunene."[15]

Evidence that a behind-the-scenes debate on Namibia has gone on at high levels of the National Party and government is also suggested by an unusual joint interview given by the ministers of defense and foreign affairs in March 1982 to Die Transvaaler, an influential Afrikaans newspaper. In a long interview, the two officials made a strong and detailed defense of the importance of Namibia to South Africa's security and for a continued South African military presence in the Territory. They argued that "SWAPO strategy in South West Africa is prescribed by the Soviet Union, and successful resistance to it in that territory is part of South Africa's struggle for survival;" moreover, a South African withdrawal would, among other things, "place the enemy closer to the heartland of the Republic," and "contribute substantially to the disintegration of South Africa's ability to withstand a full-scale attack."[16] Later, General Viljoen, chief of the SADF, warned that South Africa should not "rush into a settlement," and, should a settlement go wrong, the SADF might have to "go back in" if Namibia were "again burning."[17]

In sum, while senior South African officials may differ on specific aspects of the security threat posed by SWAPO, they appear to share a common basic conviction that a future Namibia dominated by SWAPO would pose an unacceptable risk to the security of the Republic.

How, then, did the military view the 1984 ceasefire and SADF withdrawal from southern Angola? It seems almost certain that, in agreeing to what it must have seen as a risky venture, the military would have laid down a number of stipulations, probably including its right to abort the exercise under certain conditions. SADF unease was shown by its subsequent footdragging: the withdrawal, begun 31 January, was still not completed ten months later. This delay led to Angolan complaints and several trips to Lusaka by South Africa's foreign minister in order to explain why it was taking so long for a relatively small force to leave Angola. Another measure of concern was the security forces' temporary arrest of thirty leaders of the (legal) internal wing of SWAPO in Namibia in June 1984, following a series of bomb and landmine incidents which killed twelve people.[18]

INTERNAL POLITICAL IMPERATIVES

Closely linked to the question of security is the leaders' continuing concern over political developments inside Namibia. Wrangling among Namibia's forty-odd political groupings has prevented the creation of a moderate coalition which could effectively challenge SWAPO in an election. Moreover, since political activity in Namibia has (with strong sanctions and legislative action from previous governments) developed mainly along ethnic lines, the Botha government fears that internal black politics may degenerate into tribal warfare and chaos as independence approaches. Any radical political developments or widespread civil disturbances inside Namibia would, it is feared, have serious repercussions among blacks inside South Africa itself.

Also of concern to the Botha leadership is the growing disgruntlement among Namibia's politically active white (mainly Afrikaans-speaking) community, whose right-wing political leaders already have accused Botha of preparing to "sell out" the territory's whites through an internationally approved settlement. Aktur, a coalition of right-wing white parties in Namibia opposed to such a settlement, won seventy percent of the white vote in the 1978 internal election. Aktur's major party is the local wing of the National Party. Since it has close links to the NP in South Africa, its vocal opposition to Botha policies spills over into domestic South African politics.

Deepening disaffection among Namibia's 72,000 whites has virtually closed off the option of an internal settlement and unilateral declaration of independence, an option the Botha administration, like its predecessor, strives to keep open. Nor could a divided white political leadership in Namibia provide the guidance and reassurance needed by the white community during a period of growing uncertainty and preparation for an electoral contest with SWAPO.

For Botha, however, the most serious aspect of this white disaffection has less to do with Namibian politics than with political priorities inside the Republic itself. There is little doubt that Botha considers race reform within the Republic as his government's highest priority. Yet the continuing erosion of Afrikaner support to parties on the extreme right has shown that his program of constitutional reform, modest though it appears to outsiders, remains a contentious issue in South African politics, in spite of the results of a November 1983 referendum in which more than sixty percent of the whites supported the Botha reform. If Botha is to retain enough support among the Afrikaner community and the Party to push through his reforms, prudence suggests that he must try to avoid antagonizing them over issues of lower priority. Thus, Botha has been concerned that the growing oppostion of Aktur and its Afrikaner supporters to U.N. settlement plans, as well as to the limited desegregation measures taken in Namibia, may weaken his leadership and reinforce opposition to his plans for race reform within the Republic.

Although national security and Namibian politics have been by far the major issues driving the Botha administration's policies in Namibia, several other factors have weighed significantly on its decisions.

RELATIONS WITH THE WEST

One such factor is the government's assessment of how its Namibia policy might affect relations with the West, particularly with the U.S. In the late 1970s Western leaders warned South Africa that its intransigence in Namibia was moving them toward a point where they could no longer justify using the veto to stall off U.N. sanctions against the Republic. Until the advent of the Reagan administration, South African leaders had taken seriously the threat of sanctions as a form of pressure which might be applied against either their Namibia policy or their domestic race policy, or both. The comprehensive and costly program of strategic stockpiling, armaments production, and naval preparedness carried out by successive South African governments since the mid-1960s suggests that sanctions continued until recently to be assessed as at least a strong possibility.[19] Even as late as November 1980, on the eve of the Reagan presidency, South Africa's foreign minister told a press conference in Johannesburg that "sanctions are going to come, and our people must be aware of this."[20]

In spite of South Africa's preparedness for economic sanctions, it would nonetheless be hurt by them, a fact long acknowledged by its leaders. They have therefore sought to avoid sanctions, both by making the minimal concessions deemed necessary to dampen international pressure from time to time, and by warning the world that sanctions would have a severe economic impact on South Africa's blacks and on nearby countries, as well as adversely affecting Western export earnings. In 1977, the Vorster government, in response to heavy pressure from the Western Five, cancelled its plans for an internal settlement, a move that probably cost them heavily in terms of a move that probably white Namibian unity and support.

Prime Minister Botha, however, seems to have assessed the

prospects differently, or at least to have netted out his costs and benefits differently. As already suggested, by taking a hard line against the West and the U.N. on Namibia, Botha hoped to enhance his image at home as a tough pragmatist, thereby improving the chances for his domestic race reforms to go through. Furthermore, Botha, even by the admission of his own staff, has a "super-hawkish" view of the outside world and is temperamentally inclined to accept his military leaders' notion of "total onslaught" as the guiding principle of South African policy. That view almost certainly would lead him to risk sanctions rather than make concessions which might facilitate a SWAPO takeover in Namibia. He seems also to have judged correctly that the Western powers and a number of African states, all of whom faced increasing economic problems at home, had little stomach for sanctions;[21] that they would therefore tacitly join in Pretoria's charade of illusory "movement" toward an internationally acceptable settlement in hopes of postponing U.N. action indefinitely.

Whatever concerns Botha may have had about the prospect of U.N. Security Council action were relieved with the advent of the Reagan administration, which quickly made known its opposition to sanctions.[22] In place of the sanctions threat, the U.S. now offered a conditional carrot: cooperation by Pretoria in working for an internationally acceptable solution in Namibia would open the doors for the development of a new, improved relationship with the U.S. As U.S. Assistant Secretary of State Crocker wrote in a confidential memo to (then) Secretary of State Haig, the U.S. "cannot return to 1945," but

> "We can, however, work to end South Africa's polecat status in the world and seek to restore its place as a legitimate and important regional actor with whom we can cooperate pragmatically."[23]

There is no doubt that better relations with the Western democracies, and with the U.S. in particular, are much desired by

South Africa's leaders. The question is, of course, what are they willing to pay? Afrikaner leaders normally view dialogue with outsiders not as a means of working together toward a new understanding based on mutual accommodation, but rather as an opportunity to put their case to the other party and bring him around to the Afrikaner viewpoint. For example, Prime Minister Botha readily agreed to President Kaunda's request in March 1982 for a joint meeting, noting that Kaunda was "not correctly informed of South African conditions."[24] Since the Reagan administration was more inclined than its predecessor to view southern Africa's conflicts from an East-West perspective and to make a major issue of the Cuban troop presence in Angola, this was seen in Pretoria as a welcome and long-awaited "correction" in U.S. policy. (The Botha government's so far unsuccessful attempts to maneuver the U.S. into adopting the South African view—i.e., that SWAPO and the Angolans are the advance guard for Soviet penetration of the region and that South Africa should not have been pressured into making concessions in this struggle against world Communism—are analyzed below.) In any event, the evidence suggests that Botha believed that relations with the U.S. would improve without the need for genuine South African concessions on Namibia.

COSTS AND BENEFITS

Economic factors, too, have entered Botha's calculus on Namibia. South Africa, by any account, has a substantial economic interest in Namibia. Its total investment, public and private, in the territory is more than $3.5 billion, according to a recent unofficial South African estimate.[25] A recent study by the Commonwealth Secretariat suggests that by the late 1970s Namibian transfers abroad, the bulk of which undoubtedly went to the Republic, amounted to approximately $350 million annually.[26] More important than the size of such transfers, however, is South Africa's need for several Namibian mineral products. Namibia produced substantial quantities of lead and zinc, which South Africa produces only in negligible amounts. In 1981, Namibian output of uranium ore totalled 5,000 tons, or about 17 percent of the world's production.[27] Although uranium is readily available from a number of world producers, the accessability of Namibian reserves—the world's fourth-largest—assures South African leaders of supplies for their nuclear power and atomic research programs in the event of global sanctions.

In spite of continuing concern over this issue, however, neither the government nor private industry with assets inside Namibia appears to see it as a critical problem. The official attitude is that Namibia's lopsided economy, in which mining and agriculture make up over 75 percent of the Gross Domestic Product (GDP) is critically dependent on South Africa for transport, investment capital, export markets, and budget subsidies; hence, any government in Windhoek, no matter of what political stripe, could not risk a rupture in its economic links to the Republic. Furthermore, private enterprise in Namibia already seems to have been preparing for the eventuality of a SWAPO-dominated government. In 1977, several thousand white farmers and businessmen took out SWAPO membership,[28] and by 1981, a number of foreign-owned enterprises were reported to have established legal domicile under Namibian, as opposed to South African, law.[29]

For the Botha government, by far the most serious economic concern in Namibia is the large and growing burden the Territory places on the South African budget. As early as 1982, Botha told Parliament that Namibia was "an economic millstone" around South Africa's neck.[30] In a major speech to Parliament in January 1984,[31] he reiterated this point, elaborating it with cost data. Security costs alone in the current fiscal year came to between $320 million and $400 million, he said; government aid totalled another $450 million; and government loan guarantees amounted to $550 million. Altogether, then, staying in Namibia is currently costing South Africa between $1 billion and $1.4 billion a year, or close to 10 percent of its current budget.

The Botha government's repeated statements on the heavy financial burden it bears in Namibia are clearly self-serving. In part, they bolster the credibility of South Africa's claims that it sincerely seeks and needs a Namibian settlement. At the same time, they serve as a blunt warning to Namibia's squabbling internal politicians that there is only limited time in which to organize an effective coalition before South Africa may pull out. Reminders of South Africa's financial sacrifices in Namibia also help to counter allegations that South Africa exploits Namibia economically and to suggest to the outside world that Pretoria takes seriously its self-declared responsiblities as trustee of the Territory. As Botha told Parliament, a South African departure would leave an economic vacuum which someone would have to fill.[32]

Yet there is real substance to the "millstone" statements. The Namibian economy is in a deep slump, with little prospect of significant recovery for several years. Demand for its minerals is slack, agriculture has been adversely affected by a third year of drought and by the exodus of white farmers, and a flight of capital has been accompanied by a flight of Namibian whites, who numbered less than 72,000 in the 1982 census compared to 100,000 a decade earlier.[33] There is thus little reason to expect that the Territory will be able to reduce its financial dependence on the Republic or take over more of the growing costs of administration and defense in the foreseeable future.

Meanwhile, the costs of the counterinsurgency itself appear to have grown rapidly in the past few years. The costs of maintaining a large mechanized military force, variously estimated at between 20,000 and 30,000 troops,[34] in a state of combat readiness along a distant border are substantial. This is particularly the case since the Botha strategy has called for continuous cross-border operations and frequent combined ground and air attacks inside Angola, often resulting in conventional clashes with regular Angolan units.

An additional cost of the war has been the growing SADF casualties. In mid-1979, the Defence Force reported that only one

South African soldier had been killed so far that year. In 1981, SADF deaths in the fighting had risen to sixty-one, and in 1982, the total was seventy-seven.[35] Public concern over rising casualties was evident in the spate of newspaper editorials following the deaths of fifteen national servicemen in the January 1982 fighting. A typical editorial appeared in the Afrikaans daily, Hoofstad:

> . . . although South Africans have probably become used to news of yet more deaths in the operational area, the country cannot afford to lose its young boys. The human suffering caused by such loss is indescribable, as is the cost to the country. South Africa cannot continue indefinitely with the war in South West. The premium is far too high. The search for solutions should take highest priority in this protracted South West issue, and in this the government must be supported.[36] (Emphasis added.)

In sum, then, the Botha government has come under growing pressures over the issue of Namibia. Moreover, its interests at stake in Namibia are not all congruent. Perceived national security requirements conflict with the need to achieve a settlement recognized internationally. Domestic political imperatives in the Republic—particularly Botha's plan for domestic race reform—suggest both a hard negotiating line on Namibia and the need to win support among Namibia's Afrikaner community; yet stalling on the negotiations and failure to press anti-apartheid measures in Namibia alienate its black majority, block the prospects for unity among Namibian political parties, and strengthen SWAPO's support among the populace. Postponing concessions in the hopes of gaining better terms also risks growing economic and social disruption within the Territory. And, in holding out for its optimal terms for a settlement, South Africa faces large and growing financial costs at a time of budgetary stringency at home.

How has the Botha government handled these conflicting pressures? What strategies has it adopted, and with what results?

And what can be said about the Botha administration's policy
priorities?

NOTES

1. The U.S. Memorandum of Conversation covering the talks was
   subsequently leaked to TransAfrica and published in Covert
   Action Information Bulletin (CAIB), No. 13, July–August 1981.

2. South Africa, House of Assembly Debates, Vol. 60, 31 January
   1976, Col. 361.

3. Lutheran Bishop Aula of Namibia claims that the majority of
   SWAPO belong to the Lutheran Church, which has baptized some
   300,000 Ovambo people. Los Angeles Times, 12 February 1982.

4. CAIB, No. 13.

5. Die Transvaaler, Johannesburg, 25 March 1981, cited in African
   Index, 30 June 1981.

6. CAIB, No. 13.

7. Ibid.

8. South African Digest, 3 October 1982.

9. The Star (Johannesburg), 27 September 1977.

10. The Telegraph, London, 28 August 1979.

11. South Africa, House of Assembly Debates, 24 September 1981,
    cols. 4678-9.

12. H. H. Schwarz, PFP, in House of Assembly Debates, 2 March
    1979, cols. 1710-11.

13. Paratus, April 1982.

14. From private discussion with a participant. An example of this
    occurred in early 1980, when India's General Prem Chand, who
    had been appointed by Waldheim to head the U.N. Transition
    Assistance Group (UNTAG), went to Swakopmund, Namibia, for a
    meeting with SADF officials. When two senior officers sent out
    from Pretoria "took over" as spokesmen for the SADF,

Major-General Geldenhuys, chief of the SADF's SWA Command, stalked out of the meeting in anger.

15. In a personal non-attributable interview.

16. Africa Index, 30 June 1982, p. 39.

17. Kenneth Grundy, The Rise of the South African Security Establishment, Bradlow Series No. 1, SAIIA, Braamfontein, August 1983, pp. 29-30.

18. New York Times, 8 and 10 June 1984.

19. See R. Jaster, South Africa's Narrowing Security Options, Adelphi Paper No. 159, IISS, London, Spring 1980, pp. 39-41.

20. The Guardian, 18 November 1980.

21. In an interview with the Sunday Telegraph (18 March 1979) Botha dismissed sanctions: "Personally I do not think the U.N. can apply sanctions against South Africa without hurting a lot of other members."

22. The Guardian, 8 December 1980; Kirkpatrick interview, ICA Excerpts, 23 April 1981.

23. CAIB, No. 13, p. 41.

24. The Baltimore Sun, 26 March 1982.

25. Eric Leistner, Africa Institute of South Africa, in South African Digest, 23 January 1981.

26. Roger Murray, The Minerals Industry of Namibia, (London: Commonwealth Secretariat, 1980), pp. 88-92.

27. The Telegraph, 18 May 1981.

28. Africa Bureau Fact Sheet No. 60, July/August 1979.

29. Private South African source.

30. Financial Times, 3 February 1982.

31. Embassy of South Africa, Press Release, undated (1984), Washington, D.C.

32. _Financial Times_, 3 February 1982.

33. _The Baltimore Sun_, 3 April 1982. The earlier figure, however, is somewhat suspect and may reflect a statistical error.

34. _Strategic Survey 1979_ (London: IISS, Spring 1980), p. 91.

35. South African Press Association, 30 December 1982, and _New York Times_, 19 February 1983; _Pretoria News_, 26 April and 7 May 1983.

36. _Hoofstad_, 23 January 1982.

* *

Chapter 4

THE BOTHA STRATEGY

* *

THE EMERGENCE OF THE BOTHA POLICY

No radical change in Pretoria's Namibia policy occured when P. W. Botha became Prime Minister in September 1978. Indeed, such a departure would have been surprising. For one thing, Botha, though he evidently was not Prime Minister Vorster's first choice as successor, was by no means a political maverick or newcomer to the National Party's leadership circle. To have risen through party ranks to become Defense Minister and head of the National Party of Cape Province, Botha had long since demonstrated that he was both loyal to the party and—despite some verligte notions—not too distant from the mainstream of Afrikaner opinion.

More germane to the continuity of the Namibia policy is the fact that Botha had exerted growing influence on that policy during the last year or so of the Vorster government. As the ailing Vorster was preparing to step down after his twelve-year premiership, his administration was shaken by the most serious scandal in the National Party's history. Revelations of corruption and illegal payoffs by the Department of Information—the so-called "Muldergate crisis" after Connie Mulder, the then Transvaal NP chief and minister of information—began to unfold early in 1978 and soon led to the resignation of Mulder and other high government officials. While Vorster's fading energies were concentrated on trying to contain the scandal and limit its damage to himself and his government, his hawkish Defense Minister had virtually a free hand in dealing with the growing SWAPO insurgency and with the Western Five's peace initiative. Van den Bergh, the head of the once-powerful Bureau of State Security and by all accounts Vorster's closest confidant, was himself involved in the Muldergate scandal; hence, his waning influence could no longer be brought to bear against what he had long considered the dangerous adventurism of P. W. Botha.

Botha prevailed over Ministry of Foreign Affairs reservations in the decision to launch South Africa's first deep penetration raid into Angola in May 1978: a raid which took place at a particularly sensitive stage in the settlement negotiations. Throughout the summer of 1978, Botha made public speeches in which he criticized Western and U.N. actions on Namibia, declared that South Africa would never allow the Territory to be "handed to SWAPO on a plate," and threatened to launch further strikes into Angola.[1] He indirectly criticized Vorster for his "almost painful patience" with the Western powers. In August, Botha—not Vorster—instructed General Geldenhuys, commander of the SWA forces, not to accompany a South African delegation to New York for talks with U.N. officials.[2] And, at a crucial cabinet meeting on 6 September chaired by Botha in place of the ailing Prime Minister, South Africa formally rejected the Waldheim peace proposals.[3]

Upon Botha's election to head the National Party and to take over the premiership on 28 September 1978, a leading government mouthpiece attributed his victory in part to his hard line on Namibia:

Mr. Botha's aspirations to the Premiership probably received a boost with South Africa's rejection of the Waldheim plan for South West Africa. He has repeatedly made it clear that he regards South Africa's role in SWA in warding off the Marxist orientated SWAPO onslaught as crucial. . . . It is generally held that Mr. Botha was suspicious of the U.N. plan all along . . . He said in a controversial speech earlier this month that the enemies of South Africa wanted to use SWAPO to create a Marxist state on the banks of the Orange River.[4] (Emphasis added.)

As prime minister, P. W. Botha no longer had to compete against Van den Bergh and others to win Vorster's acceptance of his point of view. Moreover, having already won the hotly contested race for leadership of the party and government, Botha no longer needed to restrain his hawkish inclinations (if, indeed, he ever did) in order to retain the support of rank-and-file party moderates. Thus, there were no grounds at all to hope that a Botha administration would opt for a softer policy line on Namibia.

Although the Botha hard-line policy on Namibia reflected no sharp break with that of the previous administration, there were nonetheless significant differences. Most obvious was Botha's increasingly aggressive and risky war strategy, which raised the level and intensity of fighting far beyond that pursued under Vorster. Botha's harder line also showed up in his diplomatic strategy. As already noted, the Vorster government had made substantial concessions to the U.N. and the West on Namibia. Since Botha came to power, no concessions of similar magnitude have been made. Indeed, Botha's growing involvement in Namibia's internal politics has been increasingly marked by concessions to the views of its white minority.

Thus, after 1978, South African strategy crystallized under the new prime minister, P. W. Botha. This is not to say his policies have always been consistent and unwavering; only that they have been marked by a hard line toward SWAPO, the U.N., and the West, and by a growing willingness to make concessions to right-wing critics at home and in Namibia. For analytical purposes, it is convenient to separate his general strategy into three parts: the war, the policies inside Namibia, and the diplomatic. In fact, the three are of course interdependent.

THE WAR STRATEGY

The Botha war strategy evolved during 1978-82, mainly in response to growing SWAPO guerrilla capabilities, a buildup of Angola's heavy weapons in southern Angola, and political developments in

Namibia and elsewhere, particularly the change of administration in
Washington. It was, however, increasingly a preemptive and aggressive
strategy, not a reactive one.

The need for this preemptive strategy was perceived only in 1978,
when SWAPO was able to begin a serious campaign of political
violence inside northern Namibia. In spite of South Africa's first deep
penetration raid into Angola in May—an attack which wiped out a
camp which South Africa claimed to be SWAPO's main guerrilla staging
area—the number and severity of SWAPO attacks continued to rise.
On 6 March 1979, Botha, who had been Prime Minister less than six
months, told Parliament of a "dramatic increase" in SWAPO terrorist
activities during January and February: seventeen cases of sabotage,
nine kidnappings of "local people" (i.e., Ovambos), twenty-four landmine
incidents, and fifteen cases of "intimidation," including the murder of
three tribal chiefs.[5] Parliament was also told that SWAPO was
receiving "extremely sophisticated weapons, and its training has much
improved." SWAPO was infiltrating in larger groups than before, and
their "anti-tracking techniques" were of the highest quality, making
them hard to deal with.[6]

The Botha war strategy was carried out with considerable
flexibility, and was adapted to changing conditions (both political and
military). Yet its overall objectives changed but little:

First, to destroy SWAPO as a credible military force. The
achievement of that objective would diminish SWAPO's political appeal
inside Namibia, as well as weaken its claims to international support as
an effective insurgent movement.

Second, to demonstrate the government's toughness in the face of
armed insurgency, and its determination not to be forced into making
political concessions because of military weakness. With the recent
Portuguese and Rhodesian experiences as worst-case models, the Botha
administration time and again reiterated its resolve to take the
offensive against SWAPO and its foreign supporters and to prevent a
SWAPO takeover under any conditions. Such a tough, aggressive
military posture would enhance Botha's domestic image in the party

and among the Afrikaner community. It was also designed to reassure Namibians, both black and white, of the government's determination to prevail over the insurgents, and thus to bolster morale and prevent a collapse of the will to resist SWAPO among white and moderate black Namibians. Further, it would place Pretoria in a strong bargaining position vis-a-vis the Contact Group and the U.N. In short, South Africa—unlike the Smith regime in Rhodesia—would keep the military option open.

A related political objective was to keep the military situation under control while seeking to strengthen moderate political forces in the Territory. The hope was to minimize the impact of the insurgency on the lives of Namibians while the Botha government took steps to build up anti-SWAPO political forces and local administrative and defense capabilities. Thus, the Botha government counted on using its vastly superior military clout to buy time while trying to establish a solid internal governmental structure in Namibia which could pursue the counter-insurgency and negotiate peace in its own name.

Another feature of the Botha strategy was to bring heavy military pressure to bear on the Angolan government as a means of forcing it to revise its policy toward SWAPO; specifically, to pressure SWAPO into making concessions in the peace talks and to discourage the Angolan armed forces from playing a more direct role in support of SWAPO.

Among the strictly military elements of the war stragegy were the prevention of a buildup of Cuban/Angolan offensive capability in southern Angola, and the creation of an SADF-controlled buffer strip inside Angola's southern border. Both of these objectives were directed toward reducing Namibia's vulnerability to cross-border attack, either by SWAPO or Angola.

In carrying out this preemptive strategy, the Botha administration initiated a broad range of tactical war measures, outlined below. Some, by their very nature, were so blatantly aggressive as to be almost certain of courting international censure, as well as risking a direct Soviet and/or Cuban military intervention.

Deep penetration attacks: Doubtless the most risky was the campaign of combined ground and air attacks against targets deep inside Angola. The early attacks were quick surgical strikes against limited targets: suspected SWAPO camps or guerrilla concentrations. But as the war with SWAPO intensified and as South Africa found that it could conduct such attacks with virtual impunity, they became heavier and of greater duration, and the tactical objectives shifted.

Thus, the first significant cross-border raid in May 1978 lasted only a day or two and was directed at eliminating a single SWAPO camp. In March 1979, following Botha's revelations to Parliament about SWAPO's growing capabilities, the SADF carried out a joint air and ground operation during which the SADF claimed to have destroyed a dozen SWAPO encampments in Angola and in Zambia, too. By year's end the number of South African troops in Namibia had risen to 30,000 from 20,000 a year earlier—an augury of heavier attacks to come.[7]

These early raids failed to stem the rise in SWAPO "incidents." Indeed, by the summer of 1980, the "operational zone" had reached the suburbs of Windhoek, and road traffic in the economically important Tsumeb-Otavi-Grootfontein triangle was forced to travel under convoy. The SADF reported that its 1980 "kill rate" of guerrillas was ninety per month, compared to thirteen per month in 1979.[8] In fact, casualties on both sides were mounting: a five-day SADF raid against a SWAPO operational headquarters in Angola during June 1980 resulted in the deaths of 200 SWAPO guerrillas and the seizure of 100 tons of weapons; sixteen South African soldiers were killed, according to an official South African communique. The growing frequency and intensity of the SADF's attacks inside Angola is reflected in official communiques of the Angolan Ministry of Defense, of which the following (excerpted from the communique of 21 February 1981) is typical:

February 10: nine SAAF aircraft machine-gunned a FAPLA (Angolan army) detachment near Ongiva, and were repulsed after inflicting "some damage and casualties;"

February 12-13: SADF troops landed from three heicopters at Mulemba with large quantities of arms;

February 13: South Africa carried out "a surprise action" 250 kilometers inside Angola; SADF forces landed at Libala, near the vital Mocamedes-Lubango railway [this railway is the site of the Cuban defensive line];

February 14: SADF troops occupied Chide with armoured cars and heavy artillery;

February 15: two columns of SADF armoured cars with helicopter support took up positions in the Ilongwe and Mulana areas;

February 16: SADF troops killed and wounded fifteen civilians in an attack near Chide;

February 21: "up to this date, South African troops are still in our territory."[9]

In the summer of 1981, following the appearance of new Angolan defense installations in the southern part of the country, both the tactical objectives and the level of South Africa's attacks on Angola moved to a higher, more dangerous level. SADF Major General Lloyd, then commander of the Southwest African Territorial Force (SWATF), warned that the introduction of an early-warning radar system and ground-to-air missiles was interferring with South Africa's capability to launch surprise ground and air attacks, its most effective means of destroying targets far beyond the border zone. He also reiterated Defence Minister Malan's 18 February warning to Parliament that the buildup of heavy weapons in southern Angola (General Malan listed 300 Soviet tanks, 350 armoured personnel carriers (APCs), and 400 infantry vehicles) meant that South Africa must prepare to face a conventional attack from across the border.

On 24 August, a few weeks after General Lloyd's warning, South African armored columns struck across the border in their heaviest and deepest incursion since their invasion of 1975. In the west, a

motorized column drove some sixty miles north to attack targets near
Xangongo (formerly Rocades), while South African jets attacked radar
and missile installations under construction in Cahama and Chibemba,
roughly 120 miles north of the Namibian border. In the east, a second
column pursued a SWAPO guerrilla band 120 miles north of the
border.

Unlike previous ground and air attacks, this one led to heavy
fighting between the South Africans and the Angolan regular army, a
confrontation which South Africa officially attributed to two new
factors: first, SWAPO had begun to locate its encampments adjacent to
regular Angolan army bases for protection; and second, although South
Africa had as usual warned Angola in advance of the attack, on this
occasion the Angolans "awaited" the South Africans and "attacked them
with premeditation" instead of staying out of the way, according to the
Chief of South Africa's Defence Forces, General Viljoen. But, in fact,
the South Africans themselves appear to have sought such a
confrontation, probably as the only way to eliminate what they
perceived to be a threatening buildup of heavy weapons in the southern
part of Angola. These included the newly emplaced radar and
anti-aircraft installations, which almost certainly were controlled and
manned by the Angolan forces, as well as tanks, APCs, and artillery,
by far the larger part of which belonged to the Angolan army, not
SWAPO.

Indeed, South Africas' aggressive intent toward the Angolan forces
was demonstrated by the results of the attack, as described and
displayed a week later by SADF leaders. Of thirty-eight prisoners
brought back, twenty-nine were Angolan regulars, eight were SWAPO
guerrillas, and one was a Soviet mechanic attached to an Angolan army
unit. The Russian was captured when the South Africans cut off an
Angolan convoy fleeing north to escape attack. A South African
commander estimated that over sixty percent of "confirmed enemy
losses," said to total about a thousand, were among the Angolans. The
display of captured weapons confirmed the fact that arms seizure was
an important objective of the attack: over 4,000 tons of arms,

including vintage T-34 and PT-76 Soviet tanks; more than 200 scout cars, heavy trucks, and other vehicles; artillery, anti-aircraft guns, 110 SAM-7 missile launchers still in their crates; and large quantities of 122mm rockets and other ammunition.[10] The South Africans' withdrawal was, in fact, considerably slowed by the staggering quantity of weapons they hauled back with them. Thus, the South African offensive of August/September 1981 succeeded in eliminating an Angolan missile complex and neutralizing Angola's heavy weapons buildup.

Sowing disruption in southern Angola: In early 1981, South Africa was revealed to be waging covert warfare, direct and indirect, against Angola. There had been little doubt, despite official denials, that South Africa was providing weapons and logistical support to UNITA, an insurgent group which has continued to wage guerrilla war against the Angolan government since losing the struggle for power in 1975. Jonas Savimbi, UNITA's charismatic leader, said in 1981 that he was then receiving "aid" from four Persian Gulf states and South Africa.[11] A U.S. State Department memorandum of conversation with the South Africans in April 1981 noted that "SAG [South African government] sees Savimbi as buffer for Namibia. SAG believes Savimbi wants southern Angola. Having supported him this far, it would damage SAG honor if Savimbi is harmed."[12] (Emphasis added.)

Savimbi claims to have some 15,000 guerrillas, of whom more than one-third have had some guerrilla training. He also claims to have broad support among the three million Ovimbundu people (Angola's largest single ethnic group) of the south central region to which Savimbi's forces retreated after the MPLA came to power. Because few outsiders gain access to UNITA's area of operations, his claims have not been verified. One Portuguese-speaking U.S. journalist who spent time with UNITA in 1977 later wrote of Savimbi's assiduous efforts to win the support of local chiefs.[13] The fact that UNITA has survived intact as an active guerrilla force, in spite of joint Cuban-Angolan counter-insurgency sweeps, suggests that Savimbi must have won considerable local support.

Yet evidence came to light in 1981 which cast doubt on UNITA's
claims of military success, and revealed just how deeply South Africa
had been involved in covert actions against the Angolan government.
Two deserters from the South African Defence Force, one British and
the other Angolan, gave the press separate and detailed accounts of
the activities of a covert SADF unit, the 32nd, or Buffalo, Battalion,
to which they had belonged. It is composed of black mercenary
troops, mainly northern Angolans who had been guerrillas with Holden
Roberto's FNLA until its defeat in 1975. It was staffed by white
officers—European mercenaries and South Africans. (More recent
reports claim that the 32nd now has only South African officers.)
According to disclosures in the British press,[14] units of the 32nd
regularly operated inside Angola, where they often posed as UNITA
guerrillas. One of their missions was local terrorism. The accounts of
the two defectors were subsequently reinforced by a report of the
South African Catholic Bishops' Conference detailing allegations of
atrocities against the Ovambo population inside Namibia:

> Reports indicate that in searching out SWAPO guerrillas,
> the security forces stop at nothing to force information
> out of people. They break into homes, beat up residents,
> shoot people, steal and kill cattle and often pillage stores
> and tearooms.[15]

Official sensitivity to such allegations was reflected in a message
to the troops from General Viljoen, commander of the SADF, in the
spring of 1982. Pointing out that "goodwill, so that locals will look to
the SADF as friends," will help win the war, he warned that

> One indiscriminate act of irresponsibility or violence
> against the local population would undo the work
> of . . . years, and . . . discredit [the SADF] and actively
> help Russian ambitions. . . . Violence against locals is
> contradictory to the policy of the SADF and where such

acts happen, strong action will be taken against the guilty parties in accordance with laid down procedures.[16]

A second covert SADF mission, again carried out while posing as UNITA guerrillas, was to fight alongside or in behalf of UNITA. As a former captain in the 32nd described it, "Whenever UNITA had operational difficulties, it would contact South African military security, which would call on 32nd Battalion to organize a force to go in and get UNITA out of trouble."[17] For such operations, he said, the 32nd would shed their SADF uniforms and regular equipment in favor of guerrilla garb and Soviet weapons, so as to avoid being identified as South African troops.[18] Western diplomatic sources have acknowledged privately that they have seen evidence of such rescue operations and of SADF contempt at UNITA's inability to hold villages which the 32nd had seized in its behalf.

Through its highly aggressive actions, both overt and covert, in southern Angola, the SADF had, by the autumn of 1981, created a buffer zone inside Angola perhaps twenty-five miles deep. In this zone, South African patrols, particularly units of the (now publicly acknowledged) 32nd Battalion, raided continuously and almost unopposed in their campaign to prevent SWAPO from establishing bases and transit camps and to intercept SWAPO units trying to infiltrate southward. In March 1982, South Africa reported that forty-five men of the "crack 32 Anti-Insurgency Battalion" had killed 201 guerrillas in an eight-hour battle to take a SWAPO base twenty-two kilometers inside Angola.[19]

Creating a Namibian defense force: An important element in Pretoria's long-term war strategy in Namibia has been to train indigenous Namibians to take over more of the fighting against SWAPO and gradually to assume responsibility for defense of the territory. The training of ethnic Namibian battalions began under (then) Defense Minister P. W. Botha in the mid-1970s. By 1979, four were operational—the 31st (Bushman), 33rd (Caprivi), 34th (Kavango), and 35th (Ovambo)—while a fifth, the 41st (Basters), was being formed.[20] A second Bushman battalion, the 201st, has since been organized.[21] At least three—the Ovambo, Kavango, and Bushman 201st—and probably others as well, have engaged in combat.

Little information has been published on the organization, training, and operations of these ethnic battalions. White SADF officers have praised individual units for their behavior in combat. It may be some years yet before these battalions can function independently, i.e., with their own officers and NCOs and under Namibian central command. As of early 1981, for example, the Bushman 201st consisted of 850 Bushmen, led by 200 white SADF officers, NCOs, and national servicemen. The Bushmen were being used as a conventional combat unit, not simply as trackers.[22]

All the ethnic units come under the Southwest African Territorial Forces (SWATF), commanded by SADF General Meiring. When this separate command was established in August 1980, the South African Administrator-General for the Territory stressed that SWATF would remain a part of South Africa's security forces until independence, and that South African authorities would retain overall responsibility for Namibian security.[23]

In October 1980, the SWA national assembly established military conscription for all Namibian males from ages sixteen to twenty-five. This move should help assure a growing flow of new recruits to SWATF's ethnic battalions. One unintended result of the new draft law, however, was the flight of large numbers of young blacks from Namibia, some of whom are reported to have joined SWAPO.[24]

Even under the most favorable assumptions, it would be a long time before the SADF could turn over to territorial authorities full responsibility for local defense. Probably that is no more than a general, long-term objective, however. Meanwhile, South Africa's leaders are creating what they hope will form the nucleus of a future independent Namibian force. A more immediate objective has been to establish a sizeable force-in-being of Namibians to assist in the counter-insurgency and gradually help reduce the number of white South African troops required to engage in combat against SWAPO and to defend the Namibia-Angola border. Indeed, these black volunteers already appear to "bear a disproportionate burden of combat."[25] Such a force could also be an important element in an international settlement on Namibia as a counterforce to SWAPO which could share security responsibilities during and after the transition to independence.

Alleging Soviet military involvement with SWAPO: South Africa has made a concerted effort to persuade the West, and particularly the U.S., that large numbers of Soviet military personnel are directly and actively engaged in SWAPO's guerrilla war. No doubt mindful of the Reagan administration's inclination to suspect all radical guerrilla movements of being part of a Soviet master plan to expand its influence by inciting terrorism and political instability, South African officials have given much publicity to the presence of Soviet and East German military personnel in Angola.[26] Their presence was hardly news, inasmuch as Soviet, East German, and Cuban military adviser APCs and technicians had been known to be attached to regular Angolan army units for several years. But a direct link to SWAPO would be something new.

Thus, following a clash with regular Angolan forces in August/September 1981, South Africa made much of the capture of a Soviet warrant officer and the killing of several other Russians as evidence of a Soviet-SWAPO military tie. Captured Russian-language documents were alleged to substantiate such charges. In fact, according to Western journalists who were later permitted to view them, the captured documents and photographs indicated that the Russians had been attached to regular Angolan army units as technicians and advisers. Some of the documents were Soviet efficiency reports on the contacts between Soviet and Angolan officers and on the advisers' progress in learning Portuguese.[27] It is of course possible that SWAPO guerrillas received training along with the

Angolan army units. Some of the captured maps appeared to show
that SWAPO guerrilla units had been located not far from FAPLA
positions around the town of Ongiva. But it seems unlikely that
training of SWAPO guerrillas would have occurred regularly or on a
significant scale, if at all. For one thing, few Angolans speak
Afrikaans or Ovambo dialects, nor are many SWAPO people likely to
speak Portuguese. Hence, joint training would be difficult, particularly
for Russians who were just learning Portuguese and had no knowledge
of local languages. Moreover, tactical training given regular army
units would in most cases differ from that required by guerrillas. In
any event, the allegation of direct Soviet military involvement with
SWAPO forces so far remains unproven.[28]

        Results of the war strategy: By the end of 1982, South
Africa's highly aggressive war strategy was paying off. Although
SWAPO was far from being eliminated as a guerrilla threat, SADF
offensive operations prevented the establishment of permanent SWAPO
bases in southern Angola. Hence, the guerrillas were forced to operate
from staging areas far north of the border. This complicated SWAPO's
logistics and reduced its opportunities to win recruits among the
Ovambo people who straddle the border (and who make up the
overwhelming majority of SWAPO membership). The heavy South
African attacks netted large quantities of arms and equipment and
probably caused up to several hundred SWAPO casualties each year
since 1979, when the deep penetration raids began. None of this can
have enhanced the morale or unity of SWAPO. Most important,
SWAPO's negotiating position in the on-again, off-again Namibian peace
talks was weakened, as was its basis for claiming to "control" parts of
Namibia.

        The maintenance of a zone of continuous operations inside Angola
also gave the SADF easy and direct access to Savimbi's UNITA
guerrillas. Direct combat support for the SADF's 32nd Battalion,
coupled with the delivery of South African arms and supplies, were
important in maintaining UNITA as credible guerrilla threat to the

MPLA regime and as a future bargaining chip in any regional peace settlement.

South Africa's strikes against Angolan missile sites and against SWAPO and (occasionally) FAPLA concentrations deep inside Angola, together with its virtual occupation of the south, increased the urgency with which the Western powers, the U.N., and the Frontline states sought a peaceful resolution. Thus, the war strategy kept all the parties engaged in the negotiating process. Moreover, since South Africa was seen to be raising the level of the conflict and increasing the risk that outside powers (i.e., Cuba and the USSR) might be drawn directly into the war, by 1981 the peace talks had come to focus largely on finding out what concessions were necessary to get South African agreement, a psychological advantage which the Botha administration exploited.

Pretoria's flagrant aggression against Angola—aggression which went far beyond even the most liberal definition of "hot pursuit"—put tremendous pressure on the Angolan government. Indeed, coping with the fighting and devastation in the south so dominated the attention of the Angolan leadership that other issues were neglected or held in abeyance. At the beginning of 1981, Angola claimed that South African attacks had caused $7 billion in damage since 1975 (this total presumably included losses during South Africa's invasion of 1975).[29] These pressures forced Angola to maintain a costly defense effort which took up half the total budget, according to an Angolan cabinet official.[30] Maintaining the Cuban "security blanket" alone is said to have cost Angola $250 million a year in hard currency.[31] Meanwhile, economic development plans were simply shelved until the end of the war.

South Africa's virtual occupation of southern Angola and its frequent attacks on towns far north of the border almost certainly exacerbated latent and longstanding differences within the MPLA leadership. Those already inclined to see Angola pursue a more doctrinaire socialist path of development internally probably also have been urging closer military and political links to the USSR and a more

militant response to South African aggression. In mid-1982, strains
were showing in the Angolan leadership, and President dos Santos
dismissed several prominent MPLA officials from party and government
posts. Western speculation[32] that this indicated a strengthening of
pro-Soviet elements seemed to be borne out in October 1982, when
U.S. and South African insistence on linking the Cuban troop issue to a
Namibian settlement led to a noticeable hardening in the Angolan
position toward the Western peace initiative.[33]

Yet moderate influences have continued to prevail. Dos Santos
has given strong support to Western peace proposals and has pressured
SWAPO into publicly committing itself to a conciliatory line. And in
spite of its military and technical dependence on the USSR, the dos
Santos government dismissed East Germans who had run the port of
Luanda and replaced them with Portuguese; moved to establish
diplomatic ties to Peking; received a top-level Portuguese economic
and political mission led by Portugal's President Eanes; and has
continued to reject Soviet advice to repudiate the Western peace plan
for Namibia.[34] The "soft line" associated with dos Santos prevailed
again in December 1983, when the angolans, desperate to gain relief
from South Africa's unrelenting military pressure, agreed to a
ceasefire. In what must have been a bitterly contested decision within
the leadership, Angola signed a formal agreement on 16 February 1984
under which its forces joined those of South Africa to interdict SWAPO
from moving guerrillas through Angola to Namibia, in exchange for a
South African commitment to withdraw its forces from Angola.

South Africa's increasingly aggressive moves in Angola also
revealed the unwillingness of the USSR, Cuba, and Angola to widen the
conflict. In spite of South African allegations, no Soviet combat
troops have appeared in Angola. The main body of Cuban troops in
Angola has been deployed in defensive positions along the
Mocamedes-Serpa Pinto rail line, which runs on an east-west axis
roughly 175 miles north of the Namibian border, well away from the
zone of regular SADF offensive operations. The Cuban defensive
posture was confirmed during the major South African penetration of

August/September 1981, when an official statement in the Cuban press
warned that Cuban forces would "go into action with all forces
available" if South African columns approached their defensive
positions.[35] Similarly, in July 1982, Fidel Castro declared that, if South
African troops "strike deeply into Angola and reach our lines, we will
fight with all our might against these parasitic, racist mercenaries."[36]
(Emphasis added.) Thus, the Cubans did not intend to fight the South
Africans in anything short of a full-scale South African invasion.
Angolan president dos Santos has stated that Angola views the southern
Africa conflicts as essentially African affairs: a clear sign of Angola's
reluctance, even under extreme provocation, to call on Cuban or Soviet
combat units to move against the South Africans.[37]

    At a tactical level, the SADF had more than four years of
offensive operations in Angola during which to develop its
anti-insurgent capabilities and to test new weapons and tactics in
combat. A senior executive of Armscor, South Africa's state-run
corporation in charge of weapons development, production, and
marketing, noted in an interview that "South Africa's weapons have the
advantage over most other producers of being battle-tested in Angola
and SWA. Prospective buyers could also be taken to the Operational
Area for on-the-spot evaluations.[38] (Emphasis added.) Indeed, there is
no evidence to suggest that South Africa's military leaders viewed the
war in Angola as a bad thing. Military budgets have remained high
and the government has been responsive to the military's demand for
improved weapons. The parliamentary opposition, as well as the South
African electorate, have accepted the military's definition of the
SWAPO threat as part of a Moscow-led "total onslaught" against South
Africa. As long as white casualties remained at a low level, and as
long as the SADF maintained the upper hand over SWAPO's insurgency,
there was no public outcry for an end to the fighting. Indeed, as
South Africa's foreign minister told the Reagan administration
privately, "It would be better to have a low-level conflict [in Namibia]
indefinitely" than to have a SWAPO regime come to power there.[39]

    One last but extremely important consequence of South Africa's aggressive strategy was to give the Angolan government a legitimate and plausible reason to keep the Cuban combat brigade on hand. This of course gave South Africa a pretext for refusing to implement a Namibian settlement. South Africa has denied any such Machiavellian intent; it claims that its offensive actions inside Angola were prompted by military considerations alone. Specifically, each major attack was justified in terms of a particular new military threat, either from SWAPO or the Angolans. The question is, to what extent were its attacks in fact determined by military/tactical considerations, and to what extent by the general political strategy of the Botha leadership and the opportunity to score political points (or prevent political points from being scored by its opponents)?

A review of available information on major South African attacks since 1978 offers some tentative answers. It suggests that some were planned and launched on the basis of military judgments; that is, their timing and stated objectives were consistent with what appeared to be the military situation at the time and the attacks cannot be clearly linked to any specific political events. Thus, Operation Protea, in August/September 1981, was preceded by numerous warnings from senior South African military leaders that new radar and missile installations in southern Angola, together with a buildup of heavy weapons there, posed a serious threat to SADF operations against SWAPO. The ensuing South African attack was clearly directed at removing these threats. Similarly, Operation Super, launched in March 1982, was aimed at destroying a new SWAPO base being constructed in Angola's far southwest corner adjacent to Kaokoland, an area of Namibia that had hitherto been immune from SWAPO activity. Moreover, in neither of these operations can the timing of the attack be directly linked to a major development in the Namibian peace talks or internal politics.

Several attacks, however, appear to have been undertaken in response to political rather than military developments. In May 1978, less than ten days after South Africa had finally agreed (following long and apparently acrimonious cabinet meetings) to accept the Western

Contact Group's proposed settlement terms, the SADF launched its heaviest and deepest attack of the war up to that time: an airborne raid on a SWAPO camp at Cassinga, some 250 kilometers inside Angola, in which South Africa reported killing several hundred SWAPO guerrillas. Not surprisingly, the raid prompted SWAPO to withhold its agreement to a settlement and to suspend the talks, which were not resumed until late summer. At the very least, South Africa's leaders must have recognized that such an attack, launched while the Frontline states were trying to gain SWAPO's acceptance of the Western peace formula, ran an extremely high risk of unravelling the painstakingly wrought settlement process.

Similarly, in October 1980, the SADF carried out what was described as a big attack—its first in four months—against a SWAPO base in southwest Angola. The attack, which went on for five days, was initiated on 21 October, the day after the arrival in Pretoria of a U.N. team headed by Brian Urquhart to discuss the composition of the proposed United Nations Transition Advisory Group (UNTAG) contingent and the status of forces during a transition to Namibian independence. The government had agreed two months earlier to the date of the visit; thus it had more than enough time to plan and execute an attack on the SWAPO base either before or after the Urquhart visit, had it chosen to do so.

Again, on 6 January 1981, the day before the opening of the abortive Geneva Conference on Namibia, South Africa was reported to have launched cross-border attacks on several villages twenty-five miles inside Angola. This attack may have been intended to preempt SWAPO from attempting a "demonstration" raid to embarrass South Africa during the conference. But, inasmuch as there is no evidence to suggest that SWAPO had any such plan, and since SWAPO's game plan at Geneva was to appear conciliatory and accommodating, the SADF attack was probably politically inspired. That is, it would demonstrate to both domestic and foreign observers that South Africa was prepared to continue carrying the fight to the enemy even while discussing the modalities of a peaceful settlement.

Operation Daisy was a combined air and ground assault on a complex of SWAPO bunkers some 150 miles north of the Angola-Namibia border. Like other deep penetration raids, it required detailed intelligence and advance logistical planning. The attack began during the last week of October and continued until 20 November 1981. Although it seems to have had a legitimate military objective, the attack may have been timed to undermine the mission of a Western Five negotiating team which had arrived in Namibia on 27 October on the first leg of a ten-day visit to southern African states.

Finally, in early August 1982, the SADF again struck deeply and heavily into Angola, killing (by its own count) over 400 SWAPO guerrillas in a sweep that lasted at least two weeks. Foreign Minister Botha had confidentially warned the U.S. in late July that a "large-scale" attack would be launched if the 15 August date for Cuban withdrawal and a Namibian settlement was not met. The timing of the actual attack well before that date coincided with important new developments in the settlement talks. In early August, a group of senior SADF officers arrived at U.N. headquarters in New York to discuss the modalities of a ceasefire and troop withdrawal, and in mid-August an advance U.N. group went to Windhoek to discuss logistical planning for the UNTAG exercise.

Unless the critical timing of these several large-scale attacks, and possibly others as well, is attributed to sheer coincidence, an explanation must be sought. First, is it likely that South Africa's military commanders, who are believed to be implacably opposed to any settlement leading to a SWAPO-dominated Namibia, would have acted independently of the Botha government by timing their attacks so as to spoil the chances of (or halt progress toward) a ceasefire and free elections? Needless to say, the evidence available on this issue is slim, and conclusions must be highly tentative. The military does, however, appear to have a surprisingly free hand in its Angolan operations. For example, an official SADF spokesman, in describing for the press South Africa's major two-weeks-or-longer foray of August 1982, said that the operation stemmed from the discovery of SWAPO documents directing that political asassinations be carried out and that arms be cached near the Namibia border; further, he said that after going in on the basis of that information, South African forces received follow-up information which took them deeper. "It was not planned in advance as a major operation."[40] This suggests that SADF leaders have the authority to decide on the ground to enlarge the scale of an operation and to move from a limited sweep along the border to a deep penetration attack. It could sometimes be to their advantage to do this, since a major operation planned in advance would require prior approval from the State Security Council, a powerful cabinet committee in which military interests are only one of those represented, though by all accounts the dominant one.

Even if it is assumed that some SADF attacks were initiated independently by the military in response to its own political perceptions, this would not apply to a number of large-scale and potentially costly strikes like the Cassinga raid of 1978 and Operation Daisy of October 1981. Both were planned from the start as heavy, deep penetration raids. Neither would have been undertaken without the prior knowledge and sanction of the top civilian leadership.

Various reasons have been adduced for these apparently politically motivated attacks. The Cassinga raid may have been ordered for domestic political effects: namely to draw attention away from the government's ostensible concessions to the Contact Group, and to preempt its right-wing critics by a show of military muscle. If those were the only reasons, the timing was unfortunate, since the raid caused a serious rupture in the settlement talks.

Similarly, the timing of the October 1980 attack and Operation Daisy in late 1981 suggests that they were designed to demonstrate that the arrival of outside negotiating teams in South Africa did not signal either a loss of will on the part of the government to pursue the war or a caving-in to outside pressure. The resurgence and growing electoral strength of the right-wing opposition to the National Party in the past few years would have been sufficient reason for a show of belligerency at such times. Aggressive actions timed to coincide with the arrival of U.N. or Western delegations would also serve to remind the visitors that the military option was not only a live one for Pretoria, but one that was being vigorously pursued. The raid on a series of SWAPO camps in March 1979 similarly appeared to convey a message to the West, as it coincided with the Botha government's strident verbal attack on Western negotiators for alleged perfidy in the peace negotiations and with Botha's threat to abandon the talks and deal with SWAPO militarily.

It is also possible that some of these coincidental attacks were agreed to by the government as a sop to the military. That is, before giving their support to what they perceived to be imminent concessions by the government, the military chiefs may have pressed the Prime Minister and the State Security Council for permission to carry out attacks timed for maximum public relations impact. The object in this case would have been to avoid giving any suggestion that the arrival of a U.N. or Western team in Pretoria, or the dispatch of an SADF delegation to New York, was a sign of military weakness or lack of resolve. Evidence of such pressure is, at best, tenuous. Senior South African diplomatic officials have been reported to express thinly veiled feelings that the military carried more weight than the foreign office in the Namibian deliberations of the State Security Council. A less direct hint of military disdain for the diplomatic process in Namibia was the statement by General Viljoen, the hawkish chief of South Africa's armed forces, that he—apparently on his own—had decided to withdraw one of his senior officers from a government delegation scheduled to go to New York because the officer was needed in the fight against SWAPO.

Finally, a separate motivation which some observers have attributed to the allegedly coincidental SADF raids is a conscious intent on the part of South Africa to prevent the settlement process from moving forward, and perhaps even to bring about its complete collapse. In this view, South African attacks were designed to provoke SWAPO into repudiating the Western peace initiative, thus freeing South Africa to go ahead with an internal solution and at the same time to avoid being blamed for the collapse of the negotiations. This view is sobering enough to warrant attention. Whether it is credible depends on how well it resonates with two other aspects of Botha's Namibia strategy: the diplomatic strategy and the moves to prepare Namibia for an internal settlement.

THE FAILED STRATEGY INSIDE NAMIBIA

Since 1977, South African strategy within Namibia has pursued one over-arching goal: to build a strong, cohesive political structure in the Territory. Through their ever-deeper involvement in Namibian politics, South Africa's leaders have sought, first, to bring together Namibia's forty-odd political parties in a moderate coalition which would offer the electorate a credible alternative to SWAPO and which would win international recognition and support. Second, South Africa has at the same time tried to establish a political and administrative structure in Namibia which could effectively govern the Territory should South Africa opt for an internal settlement.

South Africa has so far failed to achieve either objective. As the prospect of imminent self-rule led to a burgeoning of new political entities, deep and longstanding divisions in Namibian society quickly surfaced to frustrate South African hopes for compromise and understanding among the various parties and ethnic communities. A moderate coalition needs broad black support if it is to survive as a credible alternative to SWAPO. To win that support it must demonstrate progress toward ending apartheid in the territory. But Namibian whites, whose support is also needed, have been implacably opposed to desegregation. Moreover, while the major black political parties have demanded a multi-racial political structure, Namibia's whites have insisted that representation based on ethnic groups be retained.

How has the South African leadership sought to resolve this dilemma? On the surface it would seem that the interests of whites, who make up well under ten percent of Namibia's population, would have to be sacrificed in order to ensure the survival of moderate multi-racial government in Namibia. But the imperatives of white politics both in Namibia and in South Africa itself have made Botha unwilling to take a strong stand against the white minority. His policy has therefore evolved into one of temporizing and maneuver in an unsuccessful attempt to get around this basic conflict between black and white interests in Namibia.

In 1977, however, after the Turnhalle initiative had been aborted, the Vorster government focused its attention on uniting moderate white and black political groups and on winning the support of the non-white majority. Steps were taken to bypass or neutralize right-wing white parties and to harrass the legally operating internal SWAPO party. Marthinus Steyn, Vorster's choice for the Territory's first Administrator-General, acted on the assumption that he had a mandate to promote desegregation. The Democratic Turnhalle Alliance (DTA), a multi-ethnic coalition of moderate parties who had been active in the Turnhalle exercise, set out to win broad black support. With heavy financial and logistical support from Pretoria,[41] the DTA easily won an internal election held in December 1978 which was open to all ethnic groups to choose delegates to a constituent assembly.

But troubles arose for the DTA right from the start. The two major (predominantly) black parties, SWAPO (whose internal wing functions legally) and the center-left Namibia National Front (NNF) alliance, boycotted the elections, essentially because they were arranged on the basis of ethnic rather than multi-racial representation. The DTA won forty-one of fifty seats to the new constituent assembly. The remainder went to right-wing parties (six to Aktur).

Following that election, Namibian politics became both confused and fragmented. The boycott by SWAPO and the NNF ruled out international recognition of the DTA-run constituent assembly. And, since both the DTA and the South African government were committed formally to seeking an internationally approved settlement rather than an internal constitution which the outside world would reject, the constituent assembly found itself without a mission. The DTA leadership, however, was eager to turn its electoral victory to advantage and to prove itself a political force in Namibia independent of the South African government. Hence, it persuaded the Botha administration in May 1979 to declare the constituent assembly a National Assembly with broad powers of taxation and budgetary control. Executive authority in the territory resided in the Administrator–General, Judge Steyn, but the National Assembly began to establish a locally staffed civil service and to take over various administrative departments previously run from Pretoria.

The DTA leadership in the National Assembly saw that its only chance to hold the multi–ethnic coalition together and to win support away from SWAPO among Namibia's ninety–percent–black population was to move vigorously to dismantle apartheid and to improve the lot of blacks. In this it had the support, initially at least, of the Botha administration. But as the National Assembly legislated an end to segregation in public facilities, it ran into implacable opposition from Namibia's Afrikaner community, which was already strongly opposed to the international settlement (and hence to one–man, one–vote elections) to which the DTA and National Assembly were publicly committed. Aktur, the coalition of right–wing parties which had won seventy percent of the white vote in 1978, had long dominated the old Southwest Africa Territorial Assembly. But since the Territorial Assembly could no longer protect its constituents against the spate of desegregation measures passed by the new and reform–minded National Assembly, Aktur saw its power base about to crumble.

Amidst threats of strikes by white teachers and local bureaucrats against desegregation, Aktur tried to bypass the Botha government by direct appeals to Afrikaner "friends" in South Africa to tell them of the "total onslaught being waged against the National Party in SWA."[42] At the same time, it petitioned the South African courts to nullify the government act creating the National Assembly, a petition which Botha was forced to block by administrative action. Aktur also withdrew its six elected representatives from the National Assembly in protest.

This revolt of Namibia's Afrikaner community could not be ignored by the Botha leadership. But Botha was torn between two conflicting demands: that of the DTA, which could hope to win support among Namibian blacks only if it were seen to be pressing forward with desegregation, and the need to avoid alienating Namibian Afrikaners (and their kith and kin in the Republic) through being charged with selling out the interests of Namibia's whites.

The government tried to have it both ways. Initially, it tried to win broader white support for the Namibian National Assembly's desegregation measures, and encouraged the DTA leadership's initiative. It also cracked down hard on SWAPO's legal political party in Namibia, breaking up its meetings and detaining its leaders on various occasions. At the same time, however, Botha began making substantial concessions to Afrikaner opposition in Namibia. Most dramatic was his dismissal in 1979 of Judge Steyn, the Administrator-General, who had antagonized Namibian whites by promulgating a series of administrative measures aimed at reducing apartheid.

In an obvious move to slow the pace of desegregation and regain the confidence of Namibia's Afrikaners, Botha replaced Steyn with Gerrit Viljoen. Viljoen's position as chairman of the powerful Broederbond at the time attested to his credentials as a conservative and politically trustworthy leader in South Africa's Afrikaans-speaking community. Viljoen almost immediately revived the notion of a three-tiered government, with strong regional and municipal components, a scheme designed to assure whites of local control over desegregation and to weaken the more liberal National Assembly.

The strength of white opposition to the DTA's program of desegregation and eventual power-sharing with non-whites under a U.N.-supervised election was shown in the November 1980 elections to the so-called "second tier," or ethnic authorities, the legislative assemblies. Over eighty percent of eligible white voters took part in the elections to the whites' legislative assembly. Although the DTA ran a vigorous campaign with South African support, it managed to win only one-third of the votes. The local National Party candidates, campaigning for an internal settlement and elections to an ethnically based Namibian legislature, won fifty-six percent, while six percent went to parties in favor of making Namibia a fifth province of the Republic.[43]

The Viljoen administration's policy concessions to whites were reinforced by the delaying tactics of the remaining Pretoria-appointed bureaucrats who administer its laws and decrees. The resulting slowdown of anti-apartheid measures brought Viljoen, and the Botha government, into conflict with the DTA, which saw its efforts to create a strong central Namibian government structure and to move against racial discrimination being rapidly undermined. Indeed, the same series of second-tier elections in which the DTA failed to win a white mandate also showed an erosion of its black support. The Damara people, who make up Namibia's second-largest ethnic group,[44] gave the DTA party (the SWA Peoples Damara United Front) only sixteen seats in the Damara Legislative Assembly. The Damara Council party, a member of the black nationalist Namibia National Front (NNF) alliance, won twenty-three. DTA parties did, however, win six of the seven contests among the Territory's smaller ethnic groups which together account for roughly one-third of the population.

Most parties outside the DTA boycotted the second-tier elections entirely, charging that elections to ethnic bodies only perpetuated the existing ethnic divisions in Namibian politics. They also criticized the DTA, which dominated the National Assembly, for selecting the assembly's first Council of Ministers (in July 1980) on ethnic lines, and they ignored the offer of DTA chairman Dirk Mudge to add more seats to the National Assembly and to open up additional cabinet posts.[45] In the end, the several ethnic elections drew only between thirty-three and fifty-six percent of the eligible black voters.[46]

The high-water mark of DTA prominence was the U.N.-sponsored "pre-implementation meeting" on Namibia, held in Geneva in January 1981. South Africa failed in its bid to have the internal parties officially recognized as a separate Namibian delegation. Hence three

of them—the NNF, SWAPO(D), and the Namibian Independence Party—
refused to attend, leaving Namibian representation to the DTA leaders,
who came as members of the South African delegation.

Although the conference had been convened so that South Africa
and SWAPO could reach final agreement on the timing and details of a
U.N.-supervised ceasefire and elections, it was quickly apparent that
the South Africans were in Geneva for one purpose: to push the DTA
leaders into the limelight in hopes they would win status and
recognition internationally. Thus, the leader of the South African
delegation, the Administrator-General for the territory, played a
low-key role and let Mudge and other DTA spokesmen do most of the
talking. Their strident speeches, in contrast to the surprisingly
conciliatory behavior of SWAPO, concentrated on the issue of U.N.
partiality. As their price for implementing the U.N. peace plan, they
listed seven conditions which the U.N. would have to fulfill "to regain
the confidence of the Namibian people." These included rescinding the
General Assembly resolution naming SWAPO as sole and authentic
representative of the Namibian people, withdrawing SWAPO's permanent
observer status at the U.N., and ending U.N. financing of SWAPO
activities.

The failure of the conference was sealed at a private meeting of
Mudge and the Western Five Contact Group's observers, who asked
Mudge whether he would agree to implement the U.N. peace plan if
the U.N. would pass a resolution rescinding SWAPO's special status,
committing the U.N. to treat all parties equally, and authorizing a
$400 million U.N. peacekeeping force. His reply was to ask for a
delay of eighteen months. A few days later, the head of the South
African delegation delivered the official coup-de-grace to the
conference, declaring that is was "premature" to start implementing
the U.N. settlement plan.

Although South Africa's leaders later expressed, both in public and
private, the conviction that they had achieved their object of winning
international exposure for the DTA, its status was not significantly
enhanced. Observers at Geneva noted that Mudge was constantly

"surrounded" by his South African advisers, who drafted his speeches, wrote and issued DTA press releases, and were generally seen to be guiding his every move.

More important was the failure of the DTA's Geneva appearance to improve its image within Namibia. During 1981 and 1982, DTA support eroded further, as both the DTA and the National Assembly which it dominated were seen to have failed either to achieve an internationally recognized settlement leading to free elections or to make a noticeable dent in the Territory's apartheid. South African officials, as well as Namibian politicians, began to draw parallels with the Rhodesian situation, where the party representing the guerrillas had recently won a lopsided electoral victory over the multi-racial party of Bishop Muzorewa, whose internal government had been seen as a creature of Ian Smith and the white minority. In Pretoria, concern was expressed over the prospect of a "Muzorewa syndrome" in Namibia, with the DTA cast in the role of an ineffectual puppet of the Botha government. Peter Kalangula, president of the DTA and leader of the Namibia Democratic Party—the only group in the DTA representing the dominant Ovambo people—urged Mudge to move away from ethnic parties in favor of a single national party which would have greater appeal to blacks in an election campaign against SWAPO. Mudge refused. Kalangula, who was widely considered the most competent leader in the DTA, then withdrew the Namibia Democrats from the alliance (in February 1982). He invited other political groups to join him to form a new national party.

A month later, the other major coalition, the NNF, suffered the defection of its most important party, the Damara Council. This, too, was caused by internal dissension over the issue of ethnic vs. national politics in the Territory.

Not surprisingly, this political disarray in Namibia led to increasing strains between the South African leadership and the DTA. In September 1982, Botha confirmed the rumors of his growing frustration with Mudge and acknowledged that Pretoria was pressing for a more effective administration in the Territory. The National Assembly

should become more representative, he said, and a more effective
executive should be created.[47] Botha sent the head of Military
Intelligence, Lieutenant General van der Westhuizen, to Namibia to try
to reconstitute the administrative structure and bring Namibia's
forty-odd squabbling political groups together.[48]

Mudge put up strong resistance to these maneuvers, and rejected
the idea of changing the existing National Assembly and cabinet in the
absence of new elections. In November, Botha gave way and extended
the life of the assembly for three months. But in January 1983, with
a month still to go for his government, Mudge resigned as chairman of
the Council of Ministers. South Africa's Administrator-General for the
Territory dissolved the National Assembly and took over the reins of
administration.

A new Administrator-General, W. Van Niekerk, was named in
February 1983. He announced that "councils of local citizens" would
form committees to assist him in administering the Territory for an
"interim period."[49] In April, he proposed new internal elections to a
constitutional development committee which would draft a constitution
for an independent Namibia.[50] The committee subsequently became a
state council on which political parties were to draft only an interim
constitution. South African officials acknowledged privately that all
this was only to give the internal parties something to do "to stop the
place falling apart," in the words of one.[51]

Out of this council was born a new political grouping, the
Multi-Party Conference (MPC), in November 1983. Initially, it
incorporated all the significant parties in the Territory except SWAPO,
which declined to join. Members included the important Damara
Council, representing Namibia's second-largest ethnic group (ten percent
of the population), SWAPO(D), SWANU, the DTA alliance of eleven
ethnic parties, the local National Party branch, the Rehoboth
Liberation Front, and the Namibian Christian Democrats (NCDP).
Within a few months, however, the MPC suffered serious defections.
In March 1984, the Damara Council, long considered crucial to any
effective coalition, bolted the MPC, charging it with being an

anti-SWAPO front and with opposing Resolution 435. The Damara
Council then allied itself with SWAPO.[52] In April, following a split in
SWANU over continued participation in the MPC, its secretary-general
and several other party officials also joined with SWAPO.[53]

The importance of these defections became evident in May 1984,
when both the external and (legal) internal wings of SWAPO met in
Lusaka with the MPC for talks hosted jointly by Zambia and South
Africa. The South Africans had hoped the meeting would win
international legitimacy for the MPC and undermine support for
SWAPO. But the weakened MPC, encumbered with its intransigent
white-led parties (the DTA and NP), sat opposite a SWAPO delegation
that was reinforced by some sixty supporters from other parties: the
entire Damara Council, parts of SWANU and the Christian Democrats,
and representatives from the Namibian Council of Churches. This
broad array effectively demolished South Africa's longstanding charge
that SWAPO represented a small and radical group composed only of
Ovambos.[54] Three days of talks in Lusaka ended in deadlock. The
MPC failed in its bid to win a new settlement formula bypassing
Resolution 435. Nor were Kaunda and SWAPO able to get the MPC to
support a declaration calling for a ceasefire and implementation of
Resolution 435 with no reference to a Cuban withdrawal. That move
was blocked by the MPC's two white-dominated parties.

Meanwhile, the Botha government took two steps aimed at
strengthening the internal political structure of Namibia. In February
1984, Botha proposed abolishing the cumbersome ethnic administrative
authorities in favor of a strong, centralized administration. This
proposal, which was quickly accepted by the MPC parties, followed a
scathing criticism of these authorities by the Botha-appointed Thirion
Commission in 1983.[55] They have yet to be abolished, however.

By far the most dramatic move by South Africa, however, was the
release on 1 March 1984 of Herman Toivo ja Toivo, a cofounder of
SWAPO, from sixteen years' imprisonment on Robben Island. His
release had been urged by some of the MPC's black politicians in the
hope that he could be persuaded to repudiate SWAPO and to represent

the Ovambo people in the MPC coalition. This would, of course, have given a much-needed boost to the MPC as a legitimate national political alliance. The Botha government probably gambled that his release would, at the very least, cause dissension within SWAPO and perhaps lead to a split in its leadership. But none of this has happened. Toivo kept his distance from the MPC, and quickly reaffirmed his support of SWAPO and the Nujoma leadership. In August 1984 he was named Secretary General of SWAPO and was thus formally restored to a position in its top leadership.

Thus, the Botha government so far has been unable to find a formula that would respond to the conflicting demands of white and black Namibians and that would bring to Namibian politics a broad enough consensus to risk confronting SWAPO in a free and open election. In the absence of such a consensus or of a national leadership strong enough to attract disparate political groups and to submerge their differences, a further erosion of surviving alliances and a continuing drift to SWAPO are likely.

THE DIPLOMATIC STRATEGY

South Africa has been widely suspected of pursuing a policy of deliberate stalling and deception over Namibia.[56] Indeed, some African officials with the United Nations believe that, from the very start of South Africa's talks with the Western Contact Group in 1977, its leaders had no intention of relinquishing control over the Territory, but purposely set out to find one pretext after another to avoid committing themselves to an internationally accepted settlement while continuing to "negotiate" in order to keep in the good graces of the West and avoid the imposition of sanctions.[57]

There is, indeed, abundant evidence of South African stalling and refusal to "bite the bullet" on Namibia. But as a general explanation of South African strategy and behavior, it falls short on several important counts. For one thing, it is too static an analysis. It implies that South African leaders, once having set course, were not deflected by subsequent events; that over more than seven years in which talks have been going on, the dramatic shifts in South African domestic politics, the course of the counter-insurgency, the changeover in U.S. administrations, growing political disarray inside Namibia, the end of white rule in Rhodesia, and changes in the settlement terms offered—that none of this has had any real impact on South African policy. Moreover, such a consistent and unwavering policy would have required a monolithic leadership united on Namibia, as well as a basic consensus among the National Party and electorate. The "deliberate deception" argument ignores the evidence of discord within the government and party and the resulting constraints on South Africa's negotiating position vis-a-vis the Contact Group and U.N.

In fact, South Africa has yet to establish an ultimate objective in the negotiations over Namibia. In spite of the government's claims to have followed a consistent policy line,[58] no coherent plan for a settlement or for a post-independence political structure has yet emerged from the Botha leadership. The lack of such a plan reflects the government's failure to establish a consensus on Namibia, in either the Territory or the Republic. Indeed, sharp disagreements have occurred among the key constituencies weighing in on Namibia—the military, the foreign office, leading NP officials, and the bureaucracy, in particular. Available evidence suggests that they have frequently argued among themselves over particular issues in Namibia, and in some cases have taken independent action to further their own bureaucratic interests.

The absence of a strong and clear South African objective has of course affected its behavior at the drawn-out series of talks with the Contact Group and U.N. officials. Its moves have been reactive, opportunist, occasionally improvisational, and sometimes even contradictory.

Vis-a-vis its external adversaries, South Africa has been in a strong negotiating position. The pressures on the Botha leadership to avoid or at least postpone agreeing to a U.N. settlement plan have far outweighed the pressures to settle. Hence, while the Western powers

and the Frontline states have been eager to see an end to the
Namibian conflict, which has spilled over into at least two other
countries and which escalated rapidly after 1978, South Africa has been
in no hurry to settle. Furthermore, it has been more successful than
the other parties to the talks in improving its bargaining position over
time. Its punishing campaign against the guerrillas has discredited
SWAPO's claims to be an effective insurgent force and has
embarrassed SWAPO's supporters.[59] South Africa's aggressive
counter-insurgency has also put heavy pressure on Angola and, to a
lesser degree, the other Frontline states to bring the conflict to an
end. The threat to opt for an internal settlement has been another
credible bargaining chip which the South Africans have flourished from
time to time.

Yet South Africa has been unable to utilize its superior bargaining
position to extract a favorable settlement. The leadership's continuing
uncertainty over what would play successfully in Pretoria and Windhoek
has prevented its taking advantage of (apparently) extremely favorable
settlement terms when they have been proffered. Even as they have
backed away, however, the South Africans have sought to avoid or
deflect blame for undermining the talks. South African rejection of
U.N. initiatives has been accompanied by public assurances that the
door would remain open to new proposals and to further negotiations.

In spite of a limited capacity to negotiate, South Africa has used
effectively a variety of tactics to avoid an irrevocable commitment
and to win substantially more advantageous terms for a settlement.

The most frequently used tactic has been a calculated ambiguity in
South African responses. The government has agreed "to cooperate
with" or "in principle to" a Western initiative, yet has avoided agreeing
to the actual implementation. Or it has raised a general objection to
U.N. involvement, without making clear its specific objections or how
they might be alleviated. Time and again, Western and U.N. officials
have been left for long periods with no clear idea of South Africa's
position on a particular issue.

Frequently, too, South Africa has raised a new issue or obstacle to a settlement only to drop it later, still unresolved, in favor of still another new issue (or an old one revived). Since each new objection meant a new round of talks between the Contact Group and SWAPO, the Frontline states, U.N. officials, and South Africa, this tactic has stalled progress toward a settlement and has sometimes caused dissension among the U.S., its European allies, and the other parties concerned with Namibia.

The South Africans also have been keenly sensitive to political currents in the U.S., particularly the Reagan administration's obsessive concern with the Soviet threat, and have attempted with some success to seize upon issues on which the U.S. would sympathize with South African objections to the U.N. settlement plan. They have even tried, without success, to win over more conservative elements within the Reagan administration against the Crocker policy and to persuade the U.S. to repudiate the U.N. peace plan.

A further evasive tactic has been the Botha government's transparent efforts to make it appear that the decision to accept or reject the U.N. plan lay with Namibian leaders and that Pretoria would go along with whatever was decided in Windhoek. Some observers[60] have interpreted this as a legitimate move on Botha's part to place responsibility for an ultimate SWAPO-led Namibia on the Namibian leaders themselves, and thus avoid the blame, and the heavy political flak, for such an outcome. This interpretation ascribes a double naivete to the South Africans, however: a naivete on the part of South African and Namibian whites for believing that Botha would really allow the bitterly divided politicians in Namibia to make a decision with such major ramifications for South Africa's own security and internal politics, and a naivete on Botha's part for believing he could shed the blame for a SWAPO electoral victory. A more plausible explanation is that Botha's tactic was designed to win some recognition for Namibia's internal political leaders; to help them appear to be something more than puppets of Pretoria; and to strengthen his hand at the bargaining table by introducing a new anti-U.N. settlement group to be consulted on Namibia's future.

Although P. W. Botha as defense minister had exerted substantial influence on the Namibia policy in the closing months of the Vorster administration, his first opportunity to head the South African negotiating team came a month after his installation as Prime Minister. In October 1978, the foreign ministers of the Western Five countries went to Pretoria to try to persuade the new prime minister to call off or at least postpone the internal elections which Botha had recently announced would take place before the end of the year. After four days of talks, Botha would agree only to saying that the forthcoming internal elections should be seen as "an internal process to elect leaders," and that the Botha government would then "use its best efforts to persuade them seriously to consider ways . . . of achieving international recognition" through Mr. Ahtisaari, Waldheim's special adviser on Namibia, and the South African Administrator–General for the Territory. This statement is noteworthy on several counts. For one thing, it avoided tying South Africa to any firm commitment to an international settlement. Yet it also avoided committing South Africa to granting unilateral independence to Namibia based on the internal election results. Finally, it asserted that the ultimate "yea" or "nay" decision on accepting the U.N. settlement plan rested with Namibia's internal leaders, not with the South African government. This was, of course, a flimsy charade, one which has suited Botha's purposes from time to time but which was quickly dropped whenever a crucial decision had to be made. In October 1978, it was useful in suggesting that the soon-to-be-elected Namibian leaders would have real authority. If Botha also hoped that his statement would help absolve his government of its international responsibility for the Territory, he was mistaken.

Early in 1979, the prospects for a negotiated international settlement received a further setback when Botha issued a stinging denunciation of the U.N. and the Contact Group, charging them with duplicity in the negotiations and with reaching secret understandings with SWAPO and the Frontline states about the location and monitoring of SWAPO bases.[61] Talks were suspended for almost six months.

Meanwhile South Africa sharply increased the scale of its counter-insurgency war inside Angola, and took steps to organize Namibia's internal political structure.

By late summer, the Contact Group managed to revive the (still indirect) talks, which this time focused on a new idea: establishing a demilitarized zone (DMZ) sixty miles wide, straddling the Angola-Namibia border, as a prelude to a ceasefire and run-up to U.N.-supervised elections. SWAPO and South Africa both "accepted the concept" of a DMZ, although the two sides remained far apart on the details. South Africa's formal acceptance in December 1979 was hedged with several conditions regarding bases, the size of the U.N. force, and other specifics. And once again South Africa insisted on sticking to the terms it claimed to have accepted in April 1978.

Proposals and counter-proposals on a DMZ continued to dominate the discussions during the first part of 1980. This was an astutely worded reply. It did not ask the Secretary-General to show his impartiality by repudiating UNGA resolutions, but would apply only to his appointees directly involved in the U.N. operation. By May, concessions by both sides had considerably narrowed the gap between them on this issue. Since Pretoria's chief conditions had been met, the U.N. Secretary-General called on South Africa to negotiate the plan's implementation. Foreign Minister Botha's reply of 20 May neither accepted nor rejected the plan, but pledged his government to "cooperate with" it. His reply also contained an important new demand: the U.N. must end its financial aid to SWAPO, and "those directly responsible for implementing" the U.N. plan must demonstrate their impartiality. (This was an astutely worded reply. It did not ask the Secretary-General to show his impartiality by repudiating UNGA resolutions, but would apply only to his appointees directly involved in the U.N. operation.)

Thus, the issue of impartiality was introduced. This was a particularly useful issue for South Africa since—unlike more concrete issues where terms are either met or not—the criteria for impartiality had not been set forth and South Africa alone is the final judge.

Waldheim's reply to the South Africans in June promised complete
impartiality and noted that the Namibian electoral process would not
be subject to control by the General Assembly, which recognizes and
supports SWAPO, but by the Security Council, which does neither. He
called on South Africa to discuss implementing the plan for a U.N.
transition team and the status of forces.

South Africa waited two months, until 29 August, to reply. South
Africa was prepared to discuss these issues, wrote Foreign Minister
Botha, on two conditions. First, the U.N. must demonstrate its
impartiality. And second, Namibia's internal parties must be included
in all future talks. Once again the South Africans had raised a new
obstacle to a settlement.

But the new demand was not spurious or a spur-of-the-moment
issue. The previous March had seen the utter collapse of the internal
parties to the Zimbabwe elections and an overwhelming victory for the
party of the major nationalist guerrilla movement. The South Africans,
like nearly everyone else, were surprised at this result. They saw a
direct parallel in Namibia and the likely fate of the weak internal
parties in any electoral contest against SWAPO. This spurred them to
strenuous efforts to strengthen and legitimize the internal parties, as
discussed earlier. It also accounts for their stalling tactics in the
talks. Clearly, the South Africans would not risk an almost certain
SWAPO victory at the polls when Namibia's internal political leaders
were just beginning to exercise some authority. In this situation, not
even Waldheim's offer to end U.N. financial and other aid to SWAPO
and to take other measures to distance the U.N. from SWAPO had any
effect on Pretoria's position.

Indeed, during 1980, South African officials on several occasions
suggested publicly that they favored direct negotiations with SWAPO,
the Frontline states, and the internal Namibian parties in all-party
talks. In short, they loosed a trial balloon to see if there was any
support for bypassing the U.N. entirely. This bypass gambit was used
again in 1984, as discussed further on. If this was a legitimate offer
and not merely a device to sow discord among its opponents, it

probably reflected the Botha government's conviction that it could dominate such a conference and ensure a more favorable outcome than any it might gain from a settlement supervised by the U.N. South Africa did initiate secret talks with the Angolan government during 1980, but its hopes of cutting the U.N. out of a settlement failed to find support.

In late autumn, two elections took place which, together, further hardened South Africa's position against a U.N. settlement. In Namibia, the so-called "second-tier elections" to local ethnic legislative bodies resulted in the defeat of the moderate parties backed by South Africa. The right-wing white party, which opposed both desegregation and a multi-racial political structure, won fifty-six percent of the white vote, a stunning blow to Botha's hopes of uniting Namibia's varied ethnic groups behind a strong multi-racial coalition. This showed clearly that the DTA was in no position to face SWAPO in an election. Its weakness was manifest at the abortive "pre-imple-mentation talks" in Geneva two months later.

Meanwhile, the Reagan election victory in the U.S. held promise of an administration that would be considerably more sympathetic to South African interests. Indeed, South Africa's leaders, whose antennae are finely tuned to pick up even faint signals from Washington, had good reason to be pleased with those emanating from the Reagan team. Western Contact Group officials attending the Geneva conference in early January waited in vain for the incoming administration to issue a statement of support for the U.N. plan, a gesture which they hoped would nudge South Africa toward agreeing to implement the settlement. But no statement was forthcoming. Far from indicating any intent to keep the pressure on South Africa, Secretary of State-designate Haig, when questioned about Namibia during his confirmation hearings in January, said the U.S. should not "put in jeopardy the interests of those who share our values . . . above all, our interests in a strategic sense."[62] (Emphasis added.) In March, DTA chairman Mudge said his group placed "a very high premium" on

U.S. support, and that he had felt "vibrations," including statements by President Reagan, which were "encouraging."[63]

Meanwhile, peace negotiations had come to a virtual standstill in the first few months of 1981. South Africa's refusal to begin serious negotiations on settlement terms at Geneva had led to a hardening of attitudes on the part of SWAPO and the Frontline states, which called for sanctions against Pretoria and an intensification of the guerrilla war. Although the new administration in Washington moved quickly to engage the Namibian issue, disarray within the Contact Group over Washington's new approach, together with deep African suspicions of Reagan's intentions, delayed the reconvening of the Western Five ministerial group until May 1981.

Recognizing that South African intransigence was the major obstacle to a settlement, the Reagan team's first initiative was to seek ways to meet South African objections to the U.N. plan. While this was causing serious strains within the Contact Group and between the U.S. and the Frontline states, the South Africans were gratified that what they saw as their legitimate concerns over Namibia were getting a sympathetic hearing. South Africa was therefore content to follow the U.S. lead in the settlement negotiations.

The first issue was a U.S. proposal for an all-parties conference to draft a constitution for an independent Namibia. The U.S. felt that agreement in advance on constitutional principles, particularly the protection of minority rights and a justiciable bill of rights, would remove a major obstacle to South African agreement to a settlement. But this proposal flew in the teeth of UNSC Resolution 435—the only basis for a settlement to which all the parties were agreed—which called for a ceasefire and elections to precede the drafting of a constitution. The other member countries of the Contact Group, as well as the Frontline states, were hostile to the U.S. proposal. They feared it would mean dismantling the structure of agreement that had been wrought only after several years of painstaking negotiations. The South Africans, however, saw the proposal as an escape hatch from an arrangement toward which they were being nudged against their

political instincts. South Africa's Foreign Minister seized on the
Crocker proposal. Declaring Resolution 435 "dead," he called for a
new settlement plan to bypass the U.N. entirely.[64] A Contact Group
ministers' meeting on 3 May reached a reluctant compromise: they
would stay with Resolution 435 and the order of events it set forth,
but they would "build on" it by seeking the advance agreement of all
the parties on principles for the future Namibian constitution. This
issue was to be the chief item on the Contact Group's formal agenda
thoughout the rest of 1981.

Thus, from January to May, when the Contact Group's new (and
only lukewarmly supported) initiative got under way, the South African
leadership enjoyed a breathing-space during which, once again, it could
put aside hard decisions on Namibia. This was particularly important
at the time, since Botha was preparing his campaign for South Africa's
general election in May. The election was touted by all the parties as
a test of white support for Botha's blueprint for race reform in South
Africa. The results dealt a blow to his leadership, however, and were
a serious setback to his plans. Though retaining, as expected, its usual
comfortable majority in Parliament (131 of 165 elective seats), the NP
suffered a substantial defection of voters, particularly to the right-wing
parties, i.e., those opposed to race reform at home and to concessions
on Namibia. While the NP polled only fifty-eight percent of the total
votes cast compared to eighty to eighty-five percent in previous
elections, the far-right HNP raised its share from three to thirteen
percent of the total, almost entirely at the expense of the NP. Botha
defiantly declared his intention to press ahead with his race reforms.
But it was clear that his government would have to move more slowly
so as to avoid further alienating white support.

And Namibia was an issue on which white support for the Botha
leadership could erode. By October 1981, the Namibian branches of
both the opposition HNP and the NP had formally rejected the idea of
U.N.-supervised elections, and the former group had organized large
rallies among Namibian whites to denounce their "betrayal" by the
Botha government. It was therefore not surprising that South Africa

continued during 1981 to avoid making any firm commitment in the Namibian negotiations.

In spite of the Reagan administration's largely successful efforts to improve the terms on which South Africa could get an international settlement, domestic political constraints in South Africa were prohibitive. As early as June, U.S. Assistant Secretary of State for Africa, Chester Crocker, complained to a Congressional committee that, after five months of intensive talks with South African leaders, he was still uncertain if they would accept Namibian independence. A month later Canada's foreign secretary noted that "the great problem has been finding out what South Africa's position is."[65]

During the summer of 1981, South Africa launched its heaviest military strike of the war deep into Angola, but continued to discuss settlement terms informally with the U.S. Crocker told a congressional committee in mid-September that the South Africans were ready to accept Resolution 435; that they no longer were insisting on a full constitutional conference in advance of independence; and that they had accepted a peacekeeping role for the U.N.[66] In a letter to the U.S. Assistant Secretary, Foreign Minister Botha "accepted the concept" of a timetable for implementing the U.N. plan.[67]

This agreement, vague though it was, enabled the Contact Group to set in motion a three-phase negotiating process: (1) seeking agreement on a set of principles to be written into Namibia's future constitution; (2) assuring U.N. impartiality in supervising the elections and seeking agreement on the composition and deployment of U.N. forces in the pre-election period; and (3) seeking agreement on implementing the process.

Phase 1 engaged the Contact Group, particularly the U.S., during the next three months of shuttle diplomacy. The package of constitutional principles finally put forward by the Contact Group in December was designed to reassure South Africa (and Namibian whites) on minority rights and to make certain that a SWAPO electoral sweep would not lead to a winner-take-all situation leaving SWAPO in total political control. The proposal called for an independent judiciary, a bill of rights guaranteeing a multiparty system, and an end to legal race discrimination. The proposed electoral process was a complicated "one-man, two-vote" formula: half the seats in the constituent assembly would be elected on the basis of proportional representation, and the other half on that single-member constituencies. This system could prevent SWAPO from winning the two-thirds majority needed to adopt the constitution, unless it had the support of other political parties.

U.S. officials reported in late January 1982 that South Africa had accepted the proposed constitutional principles.[68] SWAPO, supported by the Frontline states, rejected the voting formula and held out for proportional representation. The talks remained deadlocked on this point until June, when all the parties agreed to bypass the voting issue and move on to the yet thornier Phase 2. The size, composition, and deployment of U.N. forces presented a daunting issue. According to U.N. and former Contact Group officials, for example, South Africa has vacillated on the numbers question, balking at an UNTAG force of 7,500 as too large, yet at other times expressing strong doubts that so small a force could effectively police the Territory during a ceasefire. The prospects of success in Phase 2 were further dimmed by the need to satisfy South Africa on the question of U.N. impartiality.

Critical developments within Botha's own party, however, had become his major concern in the first half of 1982, and appeared to have reduced his freedom to maneuver on the Namibian issue. The crucial event was the long-feared split in the National Party which finally occurred at the important Transvaal Congress in March 1982. Treurnicht, leader of the party's verkrampte wing and NP boss in the Transvaal, forced the party into an outright split over the issue of internal race reform. Botha won an overwhelming vote of confidence on the issue, after which he dismissed Treurnicht from government and Party posts and forced Treurnicht and fifteen of his supporters leave the NP. But Botha was able to do all this only with the support of a rising group of "centrists" in the Party. Andre du Toit, an astute analyst of Afrikaner politics, says that these centrists now appear to be the new powerbrokers in the Party; and since they place high value on reuniting and consolidating the Party without its far right-wingers, they will assess each issue on the basis of its likely impact on Party unity. Du Toit believes this will weaken the pro-reformists around Botha. It is also likely to have further reduced the chances for significant South African concessions on Namibia. By-elections in the first half of 1982 gave the NP only slender margins of victory, thus putting additional pressure on Botha to avoid actions that could further erode his support. For example, in the heavily Afrikaner suburb of Germiston, only a split in the right-wing vote (between the HNP and the Conservative Party) allowed the NP candidate to win. The NP polled only 3,500 votes against a combined vote of 5,200 for the two right-wing parties (August 1982).

THE "LINKAGE" ISSUE

By the time of the by-elections, South African evasion of a commitment to the U.N. settlement plan had been made easier by a new issue: "linkage." It first surfaced in a secret State Department memorandum of 7 February, leaked to the New York Times, in which the new Assistant Secretary for Africa, Chester Crocker, suggested that the quest for Namibian independence be linked to the withdrawal of Cuban troops from Angola. The issue was raised with South Africa for the first time in June 1981, when (then) Deputy Secretary of State William Clark led a U.S. mission to Pretoria to discuss the Namibian impasse. According to U.S. and South African diplomatic sources, the talks went badly. When Clark rejected South African arguments for shelving the U.N. plan, Botha lost his temper. As the talks deteriorated into mutual recrimination, the Americans prepared to leave. But they were convinced that there would be no Namibian settlement unless South Africa could somehow be brought around. In a last bid to win South African support, they asked if South Africa would be prepared to agree to the U.N. plan if a Cuban troop withdrawal were guaranteed.[69] That this had, in any event, become an objective of the administration quite apart from the Namibian issue had been made clear in April 1981, when Crocker told the Angolans that U.S. diplomatic recognition depended on the prior withdrawal of the Cuban forces. A month later, a U.S. official made linkage explicit, asserting that some commitment to a Cuban withdrawal must be part of the new negotiating framework for Namibia.[70]

(margin: in of example)

South Africa had never made a Cuban pullout a pre-condition for agreeing to the U.N. settlement plan. Indeed, publicly at least, it had never raised the issue at all. During 1981, the South Africans apparently were content to let the U.S. take the lead in pushing this issue into the negotiations. Linkage ran into strong opposition from members of the Contact Group and the Frontline states, so that by November 1981 the U.S. had refined the policy to one of "parallel movement": pressing for simultaneous progress toward a Cuban pullout and a Namibian settlement. The U.S. also reiterated its support for Resolution 435 as a basis for the latter settlement.[71]

Only in mid-June 1982 did the South Africans seize on the issue of linkage as a condition for their agreeing to the U.N. peace plan. It is not clear why they waited so long. Perhaps they thought it more effective to allow the U.S. to stay out in front on this issue and to avoid charges that it was only another South African delaying tactic. A failure to budge the Cubans would then be a failure of U.S. diplomacy, while a Cuban pullout could be used by Botha as a demonstration of the success of his hardline policy on Namibia. It was an ideal issue, too, in that whichever way it was resolved would benefit South Africa: if the Cubans stayed on, Botha would have an excellent justification—and at least the tacit understanding of the U.S.—for refusing to settle. A Cuban departure, on the other hand, would weaken right-wing forces in Namibia and South Africa who opposed a settlement, and thus would allow Botha more freedom to commit his government to the Western-led peace initiative.

In any event, South Africa used the withdrawal issue as the basis for a hardening line on Namibia in mid-1982. On 17 June, Prime Minister Botha said his government was "unwilling to complete all phases" of the settlement plan unless the Cubans departed. Further, "the Cubans must withdraw, and the strength of South African troops will be gradually reduced."[72] (Emphasis added.) A few weeks later, South Africa further stipulated that the Cubans must pull out before elections took place.[73]

Negotiations over other issues—the voting system, logistical arrangements for the UNTAG, and the composition of U.N. forces—continued, but without resolution. In July 1982, the South Africans dropped, at least temporarily, the issue of U.N. impartiality, saying that the actions of the new Secretary-General, Javier Perez de Cuellar, had satisfied them on that score.[74] But as long as the linkage issue remained alive, unresolved, and supported by the U.S., South Africa could continue to discuss the modalities of settlement without commiting itself to their implementation.

By the autumn of 1982, attitudes on linkage were hardening. Angola's foreign minister set forth his country's conditions for a Cuban withdrawal: progress in implementing Resolution 435, a ceasefire in effect, the emplacement of U.N. forces in Namibia and along the border, and a "considerable reduction" in the South African invasion threat. All this, he said, would lead to the gradual withdrawal of Cuban troops.[75] (Emphasis added.) South Africa's defense minister responded with a hardline speech before a South African business group in which he said South Africa could not accept a settlement that would result in a SWAPO victory. His further assertion, that South Africa could not withdraw from the territory because of the tactical problems this would create for the SADF, was amended a few days later to apply only to a unilateral South African pullout.[76]

As the talks dragged on without meaningful progress, renewed frictions appeared within the Contact Group. In November, the French foreign minister said that France, Canada, and West Germany all rejected linkage as a condition for a settlement.[77] It was clear that linkage had brought the talks to an impasse, and that the Contact Group was ready to break up. Only U.S. urging prevented its formal dissolution in 1982.[78]

THE NEW TRIANGULAR APPROACH

In January 1983, it was disclosed that the Contact Group's collapsed initiative had been supplanted by a new approach involving separate U.S. and South African direct negotiations with Angola. South Africa's foreign minister said his government was trying to negotiate terms for a preliminary ceasefire, while the issue of a Cuban pullout was under discussion between the U.S. and the Angolans.[79] The ceasefire talks focused on a proposed two-month freeze on all military activity in southern Angola, to be followed by the simultaneous withdrawal of South African forces from Angola and of Cuban and Angolan troops to a line 150 miles north of the border. The third step would call for an Angolan commitment to remove all Cuban troops from the country, in return for which South Africa would begin to implement the U.N. peace plan. South African officials said the issue of Savimbi's UNITA guerrillas had not been brought up. It was Angola's task to sell the package to SWAPO and the Frontline leaders.

The Botha administration was undoubtedly pleased with this new initiative, not least because it kept the U.N. out of the negotiations and engaged a relatively sympathetic U.S. administration in talks with the Angolans that paralleled those of South Africa. Indeed, in a South African state radio broadcast in December 1982, the commentator had spoken of a "joint commitment" with the Reagan administration to a "Monroe doctrine for the region," recognizing Pretoria's "special responsibility" for maintaining stability in the region.[80]

Following a discussion with Nyerere in February 1983, the U.N. Secretary-General publicly rejected the pullout of Cuban troops as a pre-condition for a Namibian settlement.[81] This position was reiterated in a U.N. Security Council meeting in June, when African states, joined by other Third World nations and the Communist countries, denounced linkage and won unanimous council approval for a resolution denouncing once again South Africa's illegal occupation of Namibia, and calling on the Secretary-General to confer with both sides about a ceasefire.[82]

This attempt to get the negotiations back under the aegis of the U.N., and thereby to kill linkage, failed.[83] The really critical talks—the only ones with any hope of progress—were the triangular negotiations among the U.S., South Africa, and Angola. During the summer of 1983, the Angolans set forth their willingness to discuss a timetable for Cuban withdrawal, conditioned on a South African troop withdrawal from Angola, the implementation of Resolution 435, and the termination of aggression against Angola, including South African aid to UNITA.[84] In August, South Africa's foreign minister, following talks with U.N. Secretary-General Javier Perez de Cuellar, declared that "all the outstanding issues" had been resolved, but that South Africa had made an "irrevocable commitment" not to implement Resolution 435 without a prior agreement on the Cuban troop withdrawal.[85]

The triangular talks led to no further accommodations until 15 December, when South Africa proposed to the Secretary-General a thirty-day mutual force disengagement to begin 31 January 1984. South African forces would begin to withdraw from Angola, provided that Angola agreed to prevent SWAPO from "exploiting" the situation. Two weeks later, Angola agreed, subject to the total SADF withdrawal from its territory and a South African promise to initiate the independence process within a fortnight of the ceasefire; this latter condition was quietly dropped as the ceasefire date approached.[86] On 31 January, Prime Minister Botha made the dramatic announcement to Parliament that South African forces had begun disengaging from Angola.[87] The details of a ceasefire were announced on 16 February, following talks between the U.S., Angola, and South Africa in Lusaka. The two opposing parties agreed to establish a joint monitoring commission to patrol the border and assure against violations by any of the forces, including SWAPO, which had agreed conditionally to accept the ceasefire for those SWAPO forces inside Angola.[88]

PRETORIA'S 1984 PEACE INITIATIVES

South Africa's ceasefire proposal reflected growing pressures on the government and a careful assessment of the military situation. In October 1983, when the U.N. Security Council voted to condemn South Africa for its continued presence in Namibia, the U.S. chose to abstain rather than exercise its veto. That abstention, together with mounting U.S. pressure on South Africa to break the Namibian deadlock, were clear indications to Pretoria that it could not count indefinitely on U.S. intervention against the growing chorus of condemnation of South African intransigence and the attendant risk of economic sanctions.

The military situation, too, had recently become more dangerous. In May 1983, Defence Minister Malan had asserted that SWAPO guerrillas were increasingly being integrated into regular Angolan units and their bases merged with those of the Angolans.[89] Whether or not this was true, the implication was that South Africa faced a growing conventional threat from across the border. In June 1983, a SADF spokesman charged that two brigades of Cubans had moved into a "chain" of bases only 130 kilometers above the Namibian border and were manning new radar and ground-to-air missile installations.[90] Although both the civilian and military leadership seemed confident that the SADF could deal with any likely threat from Angola, they also expressed their concern that the costs of the war, both financial and human, would continue to escalate.

The non-military costs of staying on in Namibia were also moving the government toward seeking an early end to the conflict. While the Botha leadership faced an internal political situation in Namibia that defied quick solution, the increasing financial burden had begun to hurt. Thus, Prime Minister Botha, in his parliamentary address announcing the ceasefire, asked the following rhetorical question:

> Can South Africa be expected to continue to bear this burden under circumstances where we do not claim sovereignty over territory, where we are exposed to criticism from the internal parties of South West Africa, where we are severely condemned by the West and where the United Nations has threatened us with enforcement measures?[91]

The ceasefire, in fact, was not all that risky a move for South
Africa. It came on the heels of a major, five-week SADF offensive,
Operation Askari, in which South African forces numbering 2,000
penetrated 250 kilometers inside Angola, allegedly to preempt a
planned SWAPO incursion.[92] Furthermore, the ceasefire was concluded
only after detailed discussions with the U.S. and, according to Botha,
"on the basis of assurances received from the United States
Government."[93] Whether those secret assurances were a guarantee of
Angolan good faith or something more has not been disclosed. But in
the talks leading to the ceasefire agreement of 16 February, the U.S.
was a direct participant. Moreover, the terms left much latitude for
South Africa to keep its security interests from being jeopardized.
When the Joint Monitoring Commission began operating on 27 February,
300 South African troops and an equal number of Angolans began joint
patrols in southern Angola, where they were soon regularly interdicting
groups of SWAPO guerrillas. Meanwhile, the withdrawal of regular
SADF units from Angola, as provided in the ceasefire, fell far behind
schedule. The original undertaking called for the withdrawal to be
completed by 31 March 1984. But in late April, Foreign Minister
Botha flew to Lusaka to explain why the movement was only
half-completed, and in June Angola's President dos Santos complained
publicly about the slow withdrawal and charged that one SADF
battalion was still positioned twenty-five miles inside Angola.[94] South
African military spokesmen charged that Angola was failing to prevent
SWAPO from moving into areas vacated by the SADF. As of March
1985, the South African withdrawal remained halted near Ongiva, about
twenty-five miles inside Angola.

The ceasefire was by no means the only new South African
initiative, however. Indeed, during the first half of 1984, a bewildering
variety of hints, statements, and secret offers—some of them mutually
contradictory—emanated from Pretoria. In March, South Africa's
foreign minister proposed a regional peace conference to be held in
Africa and attended by South Africa, Angola, SWAPO, UNITA, and the
internal Namibian political parties—in short, a move to bypass the

Western initiative and eliminate the U.N. from the settlement process.[95] This proposal, which the U.S. was not told of in advance, was rejected by SWAPO and Angola because UNITA was to have participated. A couple of weeks later, Foreign Minister Botha reiterated South Africa's support for Resolution 435, but on the day after that, Willem van Niekerk, South Africa's Administrator-General for Southwest Africa, called the U.N. plan dead since the Cubans were not leaving, and said South Africa was preparing its own plan for the Territory.[96]

In May, President Kaunda of Zambia followed up South Africa's March proposal by hosting a meeting in Lusaka attended by SWAPO and a group of Namibia's internal parties (the so-called Multi-Party Conference, or MPC). The meeting was jointly chaired by Kaunda and van Niekerk. Kaunda's hope that the two groups could agree on terms for demanding Namibian independence was dashed when the two white parties in the MPC refused to endorse Resolution 435 and raised anew the charges of U.N. impartiality.[97] The conferees could not even agree on a joint communique.

Prime Minister Botha launched another trial balloon during his European trip in June, when he said South Africa would leave Namibia if the Western powers would take over responsibility for its administration and defense. No one seemed to take this offer seriously.

At about the same time, however, reports began to leak out of yet another South African initiative, this one a secret deal allegedly being offered to SWAPO. South Africa was reported to be quietly trying to line up the support of SWAPO and African states for a regional settlement, under which Pretoria would drop its demand for a Cuban troop withdrawal in exchange for a weakening of Resolution 435 and a negligible U.N. role in the transition period. What the South Africans were offering SWAPO was nominal leadership of an interim coalition government in which such key posts as security, foreign affairs, and finance would be given to the MPC.[98] In this way, South Africa and Namibia's moderate internal poltical leaders, not the U.N., would be in effective control of the transition to independence, and SWAPO would be denied access to the levers of power.

What did this sudden flurry of South African diplomatic activity mean? Why, after seven years of avoiding a settlement, the apparent urge to settle? A major factor has been the Botha administration's new-found self-confidence: its conviction that, as the demonstrated superpower in the region, it can impose its will in the region and, together with other local states, can arrange the resolution of regional problems in ways favorable to South African security interests. This approach has been all the more appealing to the South African leadership in the absence of progress toward a withdrawal of Cuban troops from Angola, the main issue on which South Africa has felt the need for Western intervention. South Africa's specific proposals clearly show its determination to exercise enough control over the transition process to make sure that the advent of Namibian independence will pose no more than a minimal threat to South African security. Clearly, it would have far less influence over a transition in which Western powers and the U.N. played substantial roles.

The sudden urgency with which Pretoria sought an immediate settlement flowed from essentially the same set of concerns. For one thing, the South Africans hoped to extract substantial concessions from SWAPO while SWAPO was still reeling from the impact of the ceasefire accord and while its external supporters remained uncertain what steps to take to revive its waning political and military fortunes. It was a time, too, when the exhaustion of the Western peace initiative had left the U.N. at least temporarily without a live alternative in train. Nor, as mentioned earlier, were the prospects of an escalating war and growing casualties, together with the rising financial burden of administering Namibia, negligible concerns for South Africa's leaders. An additional, though less important, factor was the Botha government's perceived need to maintain what little momentum it had been able to generate behind the MPC's bid for legitimacy as a political alternative to SWAPO.

Thus, in mid-1984, a remarkable turn-around had occurred in the diplomatic negotiations over Namibia. No longer was a suspicious, truculent South Africa being pressed to agree to peace formulas worked out by the Western powers and the U.N. Instead, South Africa had seized the diplomatic initiative from them and was moving to settle the Namibian conflict on its own terms. Whether it was over-reaching its political capabilities to bring about a settlement of so complex an issue remained to be seen.

NOTES

1. **P. W. Botha: A Political Backgrounder**, South African Embassy, London, 1978.

2. Ibid., p. 38.

3. See **Strategic Survey 1978** (London: IISS, 1979), p. 88.

4. **The Citizen**, 29 September 1978.

5. South Africa, House of Assembly Debates, 6 March 1979, col. 1855.

6. Ibid., 23 April 1979, col. 4738.

7. **Strategic Survey 1979** (London: IISS, Spring 1980), p. 91.

8. **Strategic Survey 1980-81** (London: IISS, Spring 1981), p. 90.

9. British Broadcasting Corporation, **Summary of World Broadcasts**, 23 February 1981, ME/6656/B/4.

10. Joseph Lelyveld in the **New York Times**, 28 August and 14 September 1981; **South African Digest**, 18 September; **New York Times**, 2 September and 26 August.

11. **Wall Street Journal**, 17 December 1981.

12. CAIB, No. 13, p. 38.

13. Leon DeCosta Dash, Savimbi's 1977 Campaign Against the Cubans and MPLA, Munger Africana Library Notes, Issue No. 40/41, December 1977 (Pasadena: California Institute of Technology Press, 1977).

14. The Guardian, 29 January 1981; The Times, London, 30 January 1981; West Africa, London, 9 March 1981.

15. Quoted in the Washington Post, 15 May 1982.

16. Paratus, April 1982, p. 11.

17. West Africa, 9 March 1981.

18. Ibid. In response to these reports, South African military spokesmen acknowledged the 32nd's existence in the operational zone, and its international composition. But they denied that it had any links to UNITA, or a mission against civilian targets.

19. Rand Daily Mail, 17 March 1982.

20. Paratus, January 1979; Caryle Murphy in International Herald Tribune, 25 April 1979.

21. The Times, London, 9 February 1981.

22. Ibid.

23. See "Namibia: the Constitutional Fraud," briefing paper No. 2, International Defense and Aid Fund, Cambridge, July 1981.

24. Ibid.

25. Grundy, South African Security Establishment, p. 6.

26. E.g., statement by Defence Minister Malan to South African Press Association, 2 September 1981.

27. Joseph Lelyveld in the New York Times, 15 September 1981. South African field commanders made no direct allegations of Soviet-SWAPO ties. Indeed, General Geldenhuys, SADF Chief of Staff, acknowledged that such evidence was only "circumstantial."

28. Both the USSR and Angola denied that Soviet military personnel were working with SWAPO. Tass declared that its personnel in Angola "do not go beyond the boundaries of technical advice and the training of Angolan national personnel." (New York Times, 20 September 1981.)

29. Angolan Foreign Minister Jorge, interview in The Guardian, 19 January 1981.

30. Lopo do Nascimento, (then) Minister of Planning and External Trade, cited in Financial Times, 21 July 1982.

31. New York Times, 2 October 1981, interview with Portugal's foreign minister.

32. The Guardian, 16 July 1982; New York Times, 3 September 1982.

33. See Paulo Jorge statement in New York Times, 5 October 1982, and Christian Science Monitor, 7 October 1982.

34. Financial Times, 16 April 1982; Washington Post, 27 September 1982; Christian Science Monitor, 3 May 1982.

35. Reuters, Havana, 28 August 1981.

36. Washington Post, 28 July 1982.

37. The Guardian, 10 September 1981.

38. Rand Daily Mail interview, in South African Digest, 17 September 1982.

39. CAIB, No. 13, p. 38.

40. Washington Post, 17 August 1982.

41. According to Eschel Rhoodie, a high official in South Africa's information service, Vorster authorized over $1 million in 1977-78 for support of the DTA. By 1980, this support was said to be around $450,000 a month. (The Guardian, 28 March 1979; W. Johnson, "Namibia," in R. Lemarchand, ed., American Policy in Southern Africa: The Stakes and the Stance (Washington: University Press of America, 1981).

42. Financial Mail, 3 August 1979.

43. The Times, London, 14 and 15 November 1980.

44. Ovambos lead with almost fifty percent, Damaras nine percent, and whites third with just under eight percent of the total. Because of the SWAPO insurgency along the northern border, no elections were held in Ovamboland.

45. M. Clough, "From Southwest Africa to Namibia," in M. Clough, ed., Changing Realities in Southern Africa (Berkeley: IISS, 1982).

46. The Star, Johannesburg, 28 February 1981.

47. Financial Times, 15 September 1982.

48. New York Times, 27 October 1982; Strategic Survey 1983-84, IISS, London, Spring 1984.

49. South African Press Association, 18 January 1983.

50. Washington Post, 15 April 1983.

51. Ibid., 23 July 1983.

52. Africa Confidential, 11 April 1984.

53. Ibid.

54. Cape Times, 4 February 1984.

55. The Guardian, 14 May 1984.

56. See for example remarks attributed to Claude Cheysson by Tom Wicker, New York Times, 26 May 1983.

57. From private conversations.

58. E.g., P. W. Botha speech to Transvaal National Party Congress, 13 September 1982, in Supplement to the South African Digest of 17 September 1982.

59. See R. Jaster, A Regional Security Role for Africa's Front Line States: Experience and Prospects, IISS, Adelphi Paper No. 180, London, 1983, p. 24.

60. See for example "S. A.'s Bottom Line" in the The Star, Johannesburg, 31 January 1981.

61. For a detailed discussion, see Strategic Survey 1979, IISS, London, 1979, pp. 90-91.

62. The Sunday Times, London, 18 January 1981.

63. International Herald Tribune, 18 March 1981.

64. The Times, London, 25 April 1981.

65. New York Times, 22 July 1981.

66. Strategic Survey 1981-82, London, IISS, pp. 116-117.

67. New York Times, 21 September 1981.

68. Washington Post, 30 January 1982.

69. From private conversations and New York Times, 15 July 1982.

70. International Herald Tribune, 17 May 1981.

71. Washington Post, 3 November 1981; Wall Street Journal, 27 November 1981.

72. Rand Daily Mail, 18 June 1982.

73. New York Times, 6 July 1982.

74. Ibid.

75. Washington Post, 5 October 1982.

76. New York Times, 27 October 1982.

77. Washington Post, 3 November 1982.

78. Christian Science Monitor, 26 November 1982.

79. Joseph Lelyveld in New York Times, 28 and 29 January 1983; Anthony Lewis in New York Times, 2 February 1983.

80. New York Times, 11 December 1982.

81. New York Times, 11 February 1983.

82. New York Times, 1 June 1983.

83. In a major policy speech in June 1983, U.S. Under Secretary of State Eagleburger avoided the term "linkage" but reiterated the principle of "reciprocity": South Africa must leave Angola and Namibia, and Angolans "can make such steps possible . . . by assuring, as a separate sovereign act the withdrawal of the Cubans." CSIS Africa Notes No. 17, 30 July 1984.

84. Washington Post, 27 August 1983.

85. Ibid., 24 August 1983.

86. Ibid., 16 December 1983 and 4 January 1984; also Reuters, 4 January 1984.

87. Cape Times, Capetown, 1 February 1984.

88. Washington Times, 8 February 1984; Washington Post, 17 February 1984.

89. In Defence Vote Debate, reported in Rand Daily Mail, 20 May 1983.

90. South African Digest, 10 June 1983.

91. Embassy of South Africa, Press Release, Washington, D.C., undated.

92. South African Digest, 20 January 1984; Sunday Times, 8 January 1984.

93. Embassy of South Africa, Press Release, undated.

94. New York Times, 9 June 1984.

95. New York Times, 13 March 1984; Washington Post, 14 March 1984.

96. Washington Post, 22 March 1984.

97. Weekly Star, 28 May 1984; Washington Post, 18 May 1984.

98. Christian Science Monitor, 8 June 1984; Weekly Star, Johannesburg, 28 May 1984.

* *

Chapter 5

THE NAMIBIA GAME AND ITS IMPLICATIONS

* *

P. W. BOTHA'S TWO CHESSBOARDS

Political analysts find it tempting to attribute a country's policies to its leader at the time—the more so if his is a strong and dominant personality—as though all the forces pulling and shaping national policy are somehow embodied in the person and actions of the leader. This is particularly tempting in a country like South Africa. It has no tradition of open public debate over national issues, like that common to Western democracies. Indeed, its sweeping security laws discourage open discussion of anything touching on national security. The (white) electorate, especially its sixty-percent majority who are Afrikaans-speaking, have a long tradition of placing virtually unquestioning confidence and trust in their national leadership to decide foreign policy and other national issues. Since the National Party has enjoyed a more-than-comfortable parliamentary majority for over thirty years, it has been able to treat its parliamentary opposition with scorn, usually declining to engage in serious substantive debate on impending legislation. Major policy decisions are made by the Prime Minister (now State President) in consultation with the State Security Council—a powerful Cabinet committee—and a few of his closest party confidants. Often new policy initiatives catch the public by surprise.

State President P. W. Botha is said to consult more regularly and somewhat more widely than his predecessors, and he has established machinery for greater coordination among government departments and between government and industry. The military, in particular, has recently developed a strong political voice and has found ways to promote its views and its institutional interests. The formal split in the ruling NP in 1982 meant that, for the first time since it came to power in 1948, the government has had an official parliamentary opposition on its right: a highly vocal opposition of fifteen members who opposes Botha on fundamental issues of policy.

But the decision-making process remains intact. Botha and a small group of intimates, most of whom were hand-picked by him, discuss and decide policy. None of this is likely to change much under the new three-chambered parliament; indeed, the new system places more power in his hands. Since no one has ever accused Botha of being weak or without strong opinions, it can be said with confidence that his has been the dominant influence on policy in the past five years.

Botha has neither the cultural gloss conveyed by a university degree, like his Stellenbosch-educated predecessors, nor an intellectual turn of mind. He is an aggressive, articulate political animal who fought his way up through the Party apparatus, a career-type more common to the Soviet leadership hierarchy. He is said to be a stubborn man of strong convictions. His own staff say he is a "super-hawk," and his opponents in the party have dubbed him Piet Wapon (Pete the Gun) for his reputed impulsive and occasionally intemperate behavior. He has confirmed his own combativeness: "I hate weakness in public life," he said, quoting an Afrikaans proverb that "the highest trees catch the strongest winds."[1]

Botha's policy in Namibia has been consistent with his personality and style of leadership. South Africa's bold and highly aggressive military campaign against SWAPO has involved large-scale overt and covert operations deep inside Angola. In pursuing this policy, Botha has risked a general escalation of the conflict, particularly the entry of Angolan forces and the Cuban combat brigade of 20,000 or more into the war. Though the Cubans have so far remained in defensive positions 130 to 150 miles above the Namibian border, South African attacks did, in fact, lead to an increase in Angolan armor in southern Angola and to the emplacement of Cuban- and Angolan-manned radar and surface-to-air missile complexes in Angola's southern half.

The timing and scale of some South African attacks have had an adverse impact on the course of peace negotiations. Whether intended to have that effect or not, a number of the heaviest attacks were launched at critical stages in the settlement talks. At least one such attack led SWAPO to break off negotiations for several months.

Both the war strategy and South African behavior in the Western-led settlement discussions brought severe criticism of the Botha government by a number of Western powers. Indeed, frustration over what were viewed as stalling tactics by South Africa led several members of the Western Contact Group to abandon its peace initiative. Even the Reagan administration, whose policy of constructive engagement has been far more favorable to South African white interests than were the policies of its predecessors, has on several occasions threatened to disengage altogether from the Namibian peace effort in the face of repeated South African intransigence and obfuscation.

Thus, Botha has been willing to risk a widening of the war, the imposition of economic sanctions, and further international isolation of his government as Western powers abandoned their peace initiative. Moreover, in the absence of a final settlement, the internal political situation in Namibia has continued to deteriorate, and SWAPO, while prevented so far from becoming a serious military threat, seems nonetheless to have maintained its internal cohesion and its capability to carry out occasional sabotage and political assassinations. Nor has its status as the leading political force in Namibia been diminished.[2] Meanwhile, the costs of the war have continued to grow, while the need to prop up a sagging Namibian economy and an inefficient administrative structure have placed an increasing burden on the South African budget.

The question is, why has the Botha government pursued such a high-risk, intransigent policy on Namibia? Why has Botha not taken advantage of South Africa's strong bargaining position vis-a-vis SWAPO, plus a sympathetic U.S. administration since 1981, to extract favorable settlement terms for resolving the Namibian problem?

The answer has as much to do with South African domestic politics as it does with Namibia itself. Botha has been playing on two chessboards, the Namibian and the internal South African. And the latter game is for higher stakes: Botha's political survival. Botha is committed to a particular program of domestic race reform. This policy has proven to be one of extremely high risk for his administration. Already it has led to a serious erosion of Afrikaner support for the Party, and to a formal split in the Party itself. Even though his constitutional proposals, as expected, won more than sixty percent support in the November 1983 referendum among South Africa's whites, he still must contend with a large minority—perhaps close to half—of the Afrikaner community which opposes his reforms as too liberal; with liberal whites who feel the reforms don't go far enough; with a Coloured community of three million which has been sharply divided over the constitutional issue; and with the black African majority which has been excluded from the constitution and which has been organizing to oppose the reforms.[3] As the new three-chambered Parliament tests its legislative authority and as the powerful State President presides over a radically different legislative and political structure, political strains will almost certainly increase. In short, Botha's really high-risk game is the one being played on the domestic political chessboard.

By contrast, Botha's career is not at stake in Namibia. As yet, there is no significant internal political pressure on him to settle. So long as the SADF maintains a high-profile, preemptive posture against SWAPO, and so long as Botha is seen as being tough and intransigent in the face of U.N. and other external pressures, no defections from the NP ranks are likely to occur over the Namibia issue. Even in the unlikely event that Cuban combat troops were to enter the fighting, or if the political situation inside Namibia should deteriorate further, such developments would probably be seen by most whites as part of the alleged global Communist conspiracy, the well-publicized "Total Onslaught" against South Africa which some eighty percent of South

African whites have come to accept as fact.

Indeed, Botha's greatest political risk in Namibia would be to appear soft against SWAPO provocations or outside pressure, or to force integration on Namibia's right-wing white community, or, above all, to allow a U.N.-run transition to lead to an outright SWAPO dominated government. To be seen as guilty on any of these counts would provide ammunition to Botha's right-wing political opponents at home and thus would put his domestic reforms at greater risk.

Thus, the Namibian strategy, which by most objective criteria is one of high risk, is in fact a low-risk policy in terms of domestic politics. And domestic politics is the vital game for P. W. Botha.

While domestic political imperatives appear to have been by far the major determinant of Botha's policy on Namibia, at least two other influences have been important in reinforcing the hard line. A major factor has been the position of the military. Military leaders and spokesmen, from Defence Minister Malan down to field-grade officers, have repeatedly warned of growing military threats to Namibia from Cubans, East Germans, Angolans, and Russians. Frequently the threat has been magnified, and even distorted, for the benefit of domestic or foreign audiences. Military leaders have continually asserted the need for hard-hitting, preemptive, and punitive strikes, and the importance of maintaining an SADF presence indefinitely in the Territory. They have been unswerving in their opposition to a SWAPO-dominated Namibia: "No Red Flag in Windhoek" has been their oft-repeated "bottom line."

Botha's long and close association with the military as defense minister has led him to give the military establishment a greater formal role in the decision-making process. It also has meant that the military viewpoint is given greater weight in the highest policy deliberations, sometimes apparently at the expense of the foreign office position. And it is a viewpoint toward which Botha himself is temperamentally inclined.

The other major factor reinforcing Botha's hard-line Namibia policy and making South African agreement to a settlement more difficult has been the growing disarray in internal Namibian politics. In this regard, the Botha policy must be counted a total failure. The government's goal was to establish a moderate coalition of parties representing a broad spectrum of Namibia's many ethnic communities. The leadership realized that only such a broadly based grouping would be strong enough to pose a credible alternative to SWAPO in a free election. This view was reinforced by the Zimbabwe election results in 1980, when the moderate, South African-backed multi-racial coalition led by Muzorewa was trounced by the leading guerrilla group's party.

But Botha faced a dilemma which his government has been unable so far to resolve. The government-backed moderate coalition won control of a newly established Namibian National Assembly in an internal election. To win significant support from among the Territory's ninety-percent-black majority, however, the new Assembly needed to make demonstrable progress in dismantling apartheid in the Territory. When it initiated bold measures to do this, it met growing and implacable opposition from the 72,000 whites and their right-wing parties. Botha, who already was in trouble with right-wing opponents at home, proved unwilling to face up to it in Namibia. Concerned that growing white disaffection in Namibia would spill over into domestic politics, Botha effectively blocked the Namibian Assembly's desegregation program. This, together with the coalition's failure to reconstitute itself on a non-ethnic basis, led the Territory's leading black politicians to pull out of the coalition in search of alliances less vulnerable to charges of being stooges of Pretoria.

Although Botha and his military have been heavily involved in trying to establish a more durable coalition, success has remained elusive. In late March 1985 the Botha administration appeared to be moving toward establishing the MPC as some sort of interim Namibian government. Given the continuing political disarray in Namibia and particularly the dramatic shift of major parties from the MPC to a coalition with SWAPO in 1984, such a government would stand little chance of winning significant support. Meanwhile the further polarization of Namibian politics along racial and ethnic lines appears likely.

THE COMPLICITY OF OTHER PLAYERS

How has South Africa got away with its behavior in Namibia? For over six years it has been obvious that the essential missing ingredient in the settlement talks is a South African commitment to an internationally acceptable solution. Since even those directly involved in the talks, and thus those most susceptible to over-optimism about their chances of success, have been highly skeptical of South Africa's will to settle, why have the discussions gone on so long, particularly since they have cost considerable political capital on the part of two U.S. administrations, two U.N. Secretaries-General, and the foreign offices of Britain, France, Germany, and Canada?

The reasons are complex and many-layered. At the conference-table level, there was the hope on the part of the U.S. and other Western powers that, at the very least, the talks would narrow the gap between South Africa and SWAPO on specific and legitimate issues in contention. Then, when South Africa was ready to implement a settlement, the formula would already have been agreed upon and the machinery for a ceasefire, transition period, and elections could be relatively quickly set in motion. It is also likely that the Contact Group believed there were elements within the South African leadership seriously seeking a settlement; and that, as the talks progressed and various issues were resolved, these elements at some point would prevail and a settlement could be brought about. There were enough favorable, or not unfavorable, signals from the South Africans over the years to provide some basis for at least occasional optimism.

At a deeper and unarticulated level, probably all the parties involved had a strong interest in maintaining a semblance of progress in the absence of real movement toward a settlement. South Africa, of course, sought to avoid blame for sabotaging the talks, since that

would have invited global censure and pressure for sanctions. It was
clearly in South Africa's interest to keep the U.S. engaged while South
Africa tried to move the American position closer to its own. This
also gave Botha more time to deal with internal political problems in
Namibia and with the growing dissension within his own party.

The U.S., and, to a slightly lesser degree, the West European
states, also had an interest in maintaining the appearance of progress.
The Western powers wanted to avoid a nasty showdown in the U.N.
Security Council where African and other Third World states, supported
by the Communist countries, might force a series of Western vetoes on
calls for sanctions and other militant actions against Pretoria. Were
the talks to be terminated by South Africa or by some South African
action (e.g., the conclusion of an internal settlement), it was feared
that SWAPO and the African states would prevail on the Communist
governments to help them intensify the guerrilla war in Namibia. The
Western powers were concerned over the prospects and implications of
such a widening conflict which would have had serious political
repercussions at home and abroad.

In addition, the Contact Group's members recognized that a
settlement required the cooperation of Africa's Frontline states, both
to lean on SWAPO at critical moments and to sell the settlement
terms to SWAPO, the OAU, and the Third World. Frontline approval
would, in short, legitimize the settlement terms. For the U.S., there
was the further need to keep up an appearance of momentum in the
talks because both the Carter and Reagan administrations had put a
considerable amount of political capital, both domestic and
international, on the line by taking the lead in working for a
settlment.

The black African states, too, had no real options to playing the
Namibia game. The chances for a SWAPO military victory have
remained nil, nor is SWAPO likely to pose a serious threat to South
African rule in the Territory for some time to come. Thus, the goal
of the Frontline and other black African leaders has been to encourage
a negotiated settlement and the establishment of an independent

Namibia under the terms of Resolution 435. They have recognized that only the West, and particularly the U.S., can wield any influence over South Africa. (Indeed, African leaders, both in public and private statements, appear not to understand the domestic political constraints which limit what the U.S. really can do to bring pressure on the South African government.) Since only the West is in a position to lean on the intransigent South Africans, black African leaders have continually urged the Western powers to stay engaged with the Namibia problem. They fear that, in the absence of Western engagement, South Africa would move toward a permanent internal settlement; and that this, in turn, would lead to protracted guerrilla conflict with its accompanying dangers of spillover into nearby states, East-West confrontation, and continued instability throughout the region.

Moreover, even though Frontline and other African officials have been highly critical of the Reagan administration's Namibian initiative, they have acknowledged that they have no alternative solution to suggest. Their only course has been to exert continuing pressure on the Western powers to stay with Resolution 435, and to cooperate with Western initiatives by keeping SWAPO seriously engaged in the talks.

Thus, all the states involved in the Namibian negotiations have been playing the same game, though for different reasons and with different objectives. All the players have continued to support the talks, even while doubting that South Africa was negotiating in good faith, and even when it was apparent that the talks were making no progress.

The Reagan administration's insistence on linking a Namibian settlement to a parallel agreement on the withdrawal of Cuban troops from Angola has been an especially serious gamble. It reflects Chester Crocker's conviction that a Cuban pullout would remove the only real obstacle to winning a South African commitment to the U.N. settlement plan.[4] That conviction is based on several key assumptions: first, that South Africa is prepared to accept a SWAPO-dominated government in Namibia if fairly and freely elected; second, that a Cuban withdrawal would be seen by Botha as enabling him to sell a

Namibian settlement to South African and Namibian whites without either causing further chaos in Namibian politics or giving right-wing opponents at home additional ammunition to be used against him and his program of domestic race reform. Finally, that, following a Cuban withdrawal, South Africa would have no reason for further temporizing or delaying a settlement by raising other obstacles.

All these assumptions are at least questionable. Indeed, there is no basis for believing that South Africa's leaders have changed their minds about the inadmissibility of a SWAPO-dominated Namibia. Even Pretoria's mid-1984 peace overture seemed designed to undercut the possibility of an outright SWAPO electoral victory by offering it "nice cars and nice apartments . . . to play the role of South African puppets," in the words of a SWAPO official.[5] Botha's offer also showed his willingness to drop the demand for a Cuban troop withdrawal in exchange for a settlement that would leave SWAPO without effective power a watered-down Resolution 435, and a diminished role for the U.N. Thus, the real issue for the Botha government is not the removal of Cuban troops from Angola.

Indeed, from a Machiavellian point of view, Botha might really want the Cuban troops to remain in Angola, since this offers his best hope of engaging the West (the U.S. in particular) in support of South Africa in its self-declared anti-Communist struggle in southern Africa. The Cuban troop presence is also the most credible evidence he can cite to support his government's official ideology of the Communist "Total Onslaught" allegedly being waged against South Africa and the need for a "Total National Strategy," including large and growing defense budgets and a high state of military preparedness. Botha also knows that Washington is unlikely to recognize Angola as long as the Cubans are there; and since it is obviously in South Africa's interest to prevent a U.S.-Angolan rapprochement—which, in turn, could lead to a more sympathetic American attitude toward Angola and its present government—South Africa may hope, on this count, too, to keep the Cuban troops there. In short, it is by no means certain that South

Africa views the prospect of a Cuban withdrawal as being entirely to its advantage.

IMPLICATIONS

South Africa's temporizing has not only delayed a resolution of the Namibian crisis. By encouraging Namibia's diverse political groups to organize and play an active role in Territorial politics, while at the same time undermining their efforts to win broad popular support, the Botha government further polarized Namibian politics and probably made political compromise and national reconciliation more difficult to achieve. Major non-white politicians have been increasingly reluctant to place their parties and political careers at risk by joining the successive coalitions put together with Pretoria's support, particularly when these coalitions have been blocked from dealing effectively with the problems of apartheid and the war. The year 1984 saw substantial erosion of the MPC as several of its member parties joined an alliance with SWAPO. Further MPC defections appear likely, especially if the two major white-dominated parties, the DTA and local NP, continue to reject a settlement under Resolution 435 and to exhume old objections to a settlement, like the Cuban troop issue and alleged U.N. partiality.

The series of peace overtures initiated by South Africa in mid-1984, particularly the secret offer of a token SWAPO role in an interim government, show that Botha is aware of his government's failure to establish a credible alternative to SWAPO and the need to include SWAPO in any settlement that is to be durable and recognized internationally. While the initiative does suggest a certain flexibility on the part of the leadership—a willingness to consider a variety of arrangements to keep power in moderate hands—it does not indicate that the Botha government has dropped its opposition to a SWAPO-ruled Namibia. Nor does it herald a softening in South Africa's attitude toward a U.N.-arranged settlement, or a desperate urge in Pretoria to see the Namibia issue resolved at any cost.

Quite simply, the costs of Namibian administration, security, and economic support have become sufficiently burdensome to move the Botha government, for the first time, to actively seek a settlement, but one it can live with. In Botha's view, his success in forcing Mozambique to sign a mutual security pact and Angola to cooperate against SWAPO under the terms of a ceasefire have vindicated his aggressive policy toward those states for supporting guerrilla activity against South Africa and Namibia. It has also won for South Africa the recognition it has long sought as the superpower in the region. Buoyed by its military and diplomatic successes, the Botha government seems confident that it now carries enough clout in the region to pursue its own interests and its own solutions without the involvement of outside powers.

This is not necessarily good news for the West or for the prospects of a lasting settlement. It is possible, of course, that South Africa will induce the hard-pressed SWAPO leadership to settle for the trappings of power and the possibility of working within to enhance its political position. But the history of other guerrilla movements, and indeed that of SWAPO itself, suggests that tenacity and non-compromise are seen as the only sure route to power. In short, neither South Africa nor SWAPO appears to have yet reached the point of being ready to make the major concessions demanded by the other. Meanwhile, defections from the MPC have undoubtedly strengthened SWAPO's position and resolve, while weakening those of the remaining MPC parties.

Probably the greatest deficiency in Botha's Namibian policy has been the failure to develop and to articulate a coherent plan for Namibia's future political development. As suggested elsewhere in this study, this failure mainly reflects the lack of consensus in Namibian politics and in South Africa's domestic white politics, as well as Botha's unwillingness to take the bold steps necessary to win the support of Namibia's ninety-three-percent-black majority. Yet, without an ultimate objective in Namibia and in the absence of a clearly defined and consistent policy, there appears to be no basis on which to conduct rational debate, no set of propositions around which a consensus might gradually be built. Further, without an agreed government position ("No red flag in Windhoek" hardly serves as a useful starting-point for discussion), serious negotiations cannot be effectively conducted, and an internationally acceptable solution has become more difficult to attain.

Perhaps, given the wide and longstanding gulf between Namibia's dominant white minority and its black majority and among its non-white ethnic groups, political consensus is no more possible than it was in Rhodesia in the mid-1970s. And ultimately perhaps only a prolonged insurgency—one far more effective than that waged so far by SWAPO—would generate the sorts of pressure that alone might force Namibia's white minority to accept desegregation and a government of national reconciliation dominated by SWAPO.

More optimistic scenarios can of course be drawn. It is possible, for example, that a new settlement formula may be negotiated between the white-dominated parties (under pressure from Pretoria) and the growing SWAPO-led alliance, whose other members may come to exert a moderating infuence on the SWAPO leadership. But so far none of the parties to the conflict appears to be hurting enough to agree to terms that would jeopardize its perceived vital interests. SWAPO, strengthened by the return of the tough and astute Toivo, still holds out for implementation of Resolution 435, under which it would in all probability win a free election. South Africa and the MPC parties, because they also see SWAPO winning such an election, seek a settlement that would bypass or substantially vitiate Resolution 435. Such a settlement, they hope, would win international recognition and place the MPC in control of an independent Namibia, while leaving SWAPO in a nominal role. As yet no formula has been found which meets these conflicting interests.

NOTES

1. The Sunday Telegraph, 18 March 1979.

2. In a recent poll, for example, seventy-five percent of South African blacks were reported to believe that the government could not win the military struggle against SWAPO. (Cape Times, 3 February 1984.)

3. The Botha reforms involve labor law reform, manpower legislation, and the new constitution. The constitution makes no provision for black representation in the South African legislative process, although Coloured and Asians have separate legislative chambers in a three-chambered national parliament.

4. It may also reflect the administration's perceived need to make concessions to domestic right-wing critics, who would prefer to see the U.S. openly support South Africa against Marxist Angola and are more concerned with the Cuban presence than with the need for a Namibian settlement acceptable internationally.

5. Christian Science Monitor, 8 June 1984.